ABOUT THE AUTHORS

Florence T. Polatnick was born in Manhattan and attended Walton High School in the Bronx. She received her B.A. from Brooklyn College, her M.S. from Yeshiva University and her M.A. from the New School for Social Research. She now lives in Plainview, New York.

Alberta L. Saletan was born in Asheville, North Carolina and attended Fieldston School in Riverdale, New York. She received her B.A. and M.A. from the University of Wisconsin and did additional graduate work at Columbia and Yeshiva Universities. She now lives in Roslyn Heights, New York.

The careers of Florence Polatnick and Alberta Saletan have been so remarkably parallel that it is curious their paths did not cross sooner. Both received graduate degrees in economics and did editorial work in that field, then retired to raise families—each has two sons and a daughter. During their years as housewives they were active in school affairs and many civic and humanitarian organizations. Both then decided to return to work as teachers, were awarded Ford Foundation fellowships and attended the same graduate school of education. They met after beginning their teaching careers in Syosset, New York, and fruitful professional collaboration over the years led to a joint sabbatical leave during which they immersed themselves in Africana. The result was several publications for teachers and students in African studies classes and the idea for this book. They are currently devoting their extra-curricular time to in-service workshops and courses and research for a new book.

SHAPERS OF AFRICA

Africa has a rich and splendid heritage, filled with heroic figures. Spanning seven centuries, this book tells of five such leaders of varied backgrounds and talents and their achievements: Mansa Musa, ruler of the fabulous Mali Empire almost two centuries before the discovery of America; Queen Nzinga, fighter against the Portuguese conquest of Angola; Samuel Ajayi Crowther, the first black African bishop; Moshoeshoe, savior of the Basotho nation; and modern Kenya's Tom Mboya, pioneering labor leader, freedom fighter and statesman. In today's shrinking and closely interconnected world, the stories of these five leaders shed light on their times and the diversity of sub-Saharan Africa's unique and rich history.

SHAPERS OF

MANSA MUSA
MALI EMPIRE

QUEEN NZINGA
ANGOLA

SAMUEL AJAYI CROWTHER
NIGERIA

MOSHOESHOE
LESOTHO

TOM MBOYA
KENYA

AFRICA

Florence T. Polatnick
and
Alberta L. Saletan

Maps and Illustrations

JLIAN MESSNER NEW YORK

CREDITS

From ISLAM by Muhammed Zafrulla Khan. Copyright © 1962 by Muhammed Zafrulla Khan. Reprinted by permission of Harper & Row, Publishers.

Angola in Perspective by F. Clement C. Egerton. Published by Routledge & Kegan Paul Ltd., 1957.

Salvador de Sa by Professor C. R. Boxer. Published by The Athlone Press of the University of London, 1952.

Eminent Nigerians of the 19th Century by F. O. Dike. Published by Cambridge University Press, 1960. Also courtesy the Nigerian Broadcasting Corporation.

Moshesh—The Man on the Mountain by J. Grenfell Williams.

The Washing of Spears by Donald R. Morris. Copyright © 1965 by Donald R. Morris. Published by Simon & Schuster, Inc.

A History of Postwar Africa by John Hatch. Published by Frederick A. Praeger, Inc., 1965.

Freedom and After by Tom Mboya. Copyright © 1963 by Tom Mboya. By permission of Little, Brown and Co.

"Do White Men Have a Future in Africa?" by Tom Mboya. *The New York Times Magazine, December 8, 1963.* © 1963 by The New York Times Company. Reprinted by permission. Also courtesy Thomas J. Mboya.

From TOM MBOYA by Alan Rake. Copyright © 1962 by Alan Rake. Reprinted by permission of Doubleday & Company, Inc. Also courtesy John Farquharson Ltd.

Printed in the United States of America.

SBN 671-32193-5 Cloth Trade
      671-32194-3 MCE

Library of Congress Catalog Card No. 76-83149

FOREWORD

If the names of Napoleon, Abraham Lincoln and Pope John XXIII are mentioned to most Americans, there is no need to explain further. But a reference to Mansa Musa, Moshoeshoe or Bishop Crowther is likely to be met with the statement, "Who is that? I never heard of him." The reasons for this ignorance of great figures of the African past are not difficult to find. Africa's history was preserved through an oral tradition, tribal lore handed down through the generations by word of mouth. When Africa's story was finally written down, it was the invading Arabs or Europeans who penned the history—and added their particular biases. Until recently, Americans learned little or nothing in school about the non-Western world. The heroes and villains of our history books were either American or European, as though the rest of the world had no history with heroes and villains of its own. Then, when Asia and Africa began to be part of the course of study, attention was focused only on the colonial period, a brief segment of their total history. It is only now, in today's shrinking and closely interconnected world, that our schools have begun to recognize that each part of the earth has its own unique and rich history.

On every continent, civilizations have flourished with their own special qualities, their particular successes and failures, their varying periods of influence. Each of these civilizations has produced many different kinds of people—leaders, followers, wise men, fools, good men, rogues. Some of the outstanding figures become enshrined in legend or history; others have a moment of glory and are forgotten.

Africa, of course, shares this common human past and present. This book of short biographies can serve only to give the reader a glimpse of those who people the pages of African history. The subjects have been chosen from a time span of almost 700 years to illustrate the diversity and range of human endeavor in sub-Saharan Africa. There is Mansa Musa, the great conqueror and administrator, devout son of Islam; Queen Nzinga, the valiant and tenacious freedom fighter; Samuel Ajayi Crowther, gentle bishop; Moshoeshoe, the father of his country; Tom Mboya, contemporary labor leader and skilled political activist. Each of these significant leaders illuminates both his individual time and our understanding of how human greatness flourishes in a cultural setting different from our own.

  Because there are few written accounts of much of sub-Saharan Africa's past, it is often impossible to obtain a complete and accurate record of a particular person and his epoch. The lives of our heroes have been reconstructed from the available research sources, in full recognition that there are unavoidable gaps and a number of possible interpretations. It is the authors' hope that this effort to bring five outstanding Africans to life will offer the reader a fresh insight into the common human qualities of all men in all societies.

ACKNOWLEDGMENTS

We wish to acknowledge with thanks the helpful assistance of the staff at the Central Building and the Schomburg Branch of the New York Public Library, the Widener Library at Harvard University, the Mugar Memorial Library at Boston University and the Plainview–Old Bethpage Public Library in Long Island.

We are also particularly grateful to Professor Khalil A. Nasir and to Mr. Vincent Malebo, Chief Counselor of the Lesotho Mission to the United Nations, both of whom helped resolve problems of transliteration of language. Mrs. Martha M. Lebotsa, Chief Archivist of the Government of Lesotho, was a valuable source of information on the history of Moshoeshoe and the Basotho people.

Florence T. Polatnick
Alberta L. Saletan

CONTENTS

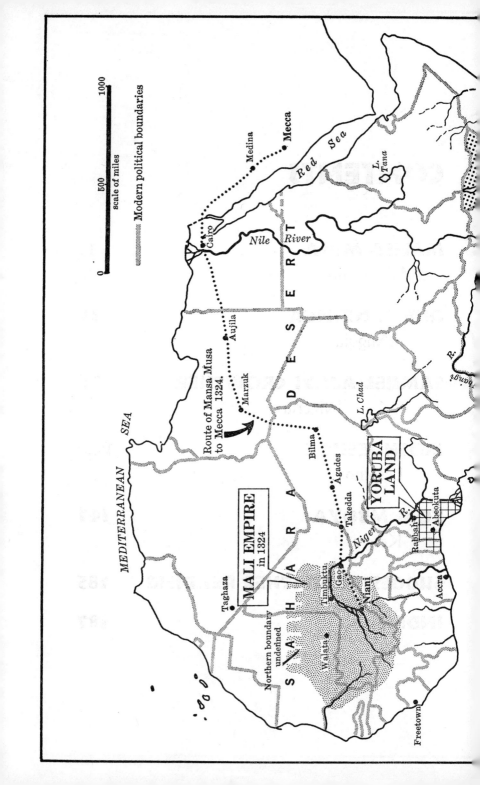

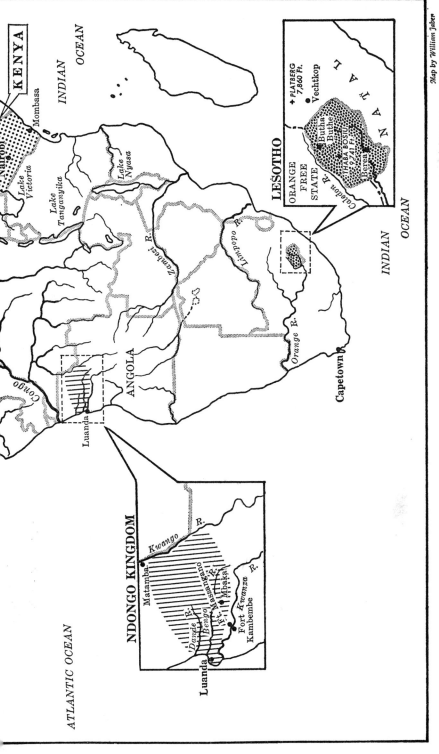

ATLANTIC OCEAN

NDONGO KINGDOM

Kwango R.
Matamba
Dande R.
Bengo
Massangano
Ft.
Mbaka
Fort Kwanza
Kambembe R.
Luanda

KENYA

INDIAN OCEAN

Nairobi
Mombasa
Lake Victoria
Lake Tanganyika
Lake Nyasa

Congo
Zambezi R.
ANGOLA
Luanda
Limpopo R.
Orange R.
Capetown

LESOTHO

ORANGE FREE STATE

NATAL

INDIAN OCEAN

Caledon R.
PLATBERG 7,860 Ft.
Vechtkop
Butha Buthe
THABA BOSIU 9,741 Ft.
Berea

Map by William Jaber

MANSA MUSA

"PEACE be on you and the mercy of God and his blessings." The Emperor's messenger bowed deeply to the governor and his aides assembled in the courtyard. "I bring word from Mansa Musa, our noble lord and ruler, to his faithful servants throughout the land. Know, then, that in fulfillment of his duty as a devout Moslem, our sovereign will travel to Mecca, the holy city, to worship at the Temple of Abraham."

A buzz of excitement whipped through the air as the officials began to murmur to each other. "Mansa Musa will make the pilgrimage—an immense journey!" "Perhaps he will take some of us."

The governor raised a hand to still the voices. "I hear the news of our master's journey and I rejoice," he said to the messenger. "When does the pilgrimage take place?"

"When all has been prepared," replied the messenger. "Our Emperor requires that you and all the governors of the provinces of Mali begin to gather supplies for the journey at once. Much will be needed, and the tribute regularly collected will not suffice. All governors and the local chiefs subject to them must redouble their efforts."

"I hear the voice of the Emperor, and it brings me joy to obey. What are my orders?" asked the governor.

"You, oh *farba* [governor], are to send your men to every farm in every village. The Emperor must have grain, calabashes, rice, yams—enough to supply the most glorious caravan ever to cross the burning desert. Your weavers must make cloth for the pilgrims' garments; your blacksmiths, lances to defend the faithful; your leather craftsmen, saddles and harness. Each man in the kingdom shall share in the honor of providing for our master's journey."

"It shall be as Mansa Musa wills." The governor stared thoughtfully at the messenger and then added, "Who will accompany our sovereign on the pilgrimage?"

"I do not know," responded the messenger. "The Emperor will reveal his pleasure when the time draws near. In the meantime, let there be no delay in collecting your province's gifts. Our master grows impatient to begin the holy journey."

The great Mali Empire of the early 1300s was indeed well suited for the organization of the spectacular pilgrimage being planned by the Emperor of the Mandingo people. While there are no firsthand reports by inhabitants or travelers in Mansa Musa's kingdom, much has been learned from the writings of Arabs who came to Mali after the Emperor's death or who talked with those who had seen the Empire themselves. The exact boundaries of Mali at the height of its power are not known, but it is clear that the Empire covered a huge territory. From the capital city of Niani, probably located on the Sankarini River (a tributary of the Niger), the kingdom stretched almost a thousand miles north into the blazing Sahara, past the great salt deposits of Taghaza. Eastward about the same distance lay the caravan center of Takedda, whose rich copper mines led Mansa Musa to comment that this was his most important source of income, since copper could be sold for two-thirds of its weight in gold. Southward Mali reached the edges of the dense coastal forests, and westward the restless waters of the Atlantic Ocean.

Wealth was the hallmark of the Empire. The fertile fields of Mali, lying in the flood plain of the Niger River and on the rich plateau between the Niger and the Senegal, yielded abundant crops. From the mysterious forests of the Wangara people, gold in seemingly limitless supply flowed into the coffers of the Mansa, who had sole right to all the precious metal in the kingdom. The Berber sultan of Takedda, vassal to Mansa Musa, provided the copper which his sweating slaves cast in their mud houses. Rock salt in huge slabs, a vital necessity for the Sudan, which had no salt of its own, came from the Saharan mines at the far edges of the Empire. To exchange their products for these riches, caravans from the Mediterranean shores of the Maghreb and from Egypt, at the other end of the continent, passed in endless procession through the bustling towns of Mali.

The great Empire, approximately the size of Western Europe,

had been forged during the 13th century. The Mandingo people, then weak and scattered, had rallied to the powerful leadership of Sundiata, who became king of the small Mandingo state of Mali in 1230 A.D. The army raised by Sundiata thrust forward under his conquering banner, pushing the boundaries of Mali ever further. The little kingdom mushroomed into an expanding empire, with the newly defeated territories paying regular tribute to the emperor.

The rulers of Mali who followed Sundiata extended his conquests and continued the complex task of organizing the economy and government of the growing empire. But it was left to Mansa Musa, great-nephew of Sundiata, to bring the empire to its greatest hour of glory and vigor.

Throughout the kingdom of Mali during the year of 1324 the envoys of Mansa Musa (Arabic for "Emperor Moses") carried the word of their ruler's decision to set out on the holy pilgrimage to Mecca. The kings of the Mandingo people had been converted to Islam by the Almoravid invaders who had swept down from the north during the 11th century. While many of the Mandingo people retained their own earlier religious beliefs, the members of the royal house and their entourage had long been devout Moslems. The deep piety of Mansa Musa, whose forebears had been faithful followers of the Prophet for nearly three centuries, found its natural expression in his determination to make the pilgrimage.

From one end of the western Sudan to the other, wherever the immense power of the Empire of Mali cast its shadow, men toiled to provide supplies for the huge caravan slowly being assembled at Niani, the capital city. In the provinces, where Mansa Musa's generals and governors vied to outdo one another in their fierce loyalty to their ruler, goods were piled high awaiting the arrival of camel trains for transport to Niani. In the score of semi-independent kingdoms which paid tribute to the Mandingo emperor, the local kings and chiefs, well aware

of the price they would have to pay if they failed in their
duty, spurred their people to ever-increasing efforts in farming
and artisanship.

At home in his palace, Mansa Musa reflected on his coming
hadj, the journey to the holy city of Mecca which each Moslem
must make, if he is able, once during his lifetime. I have sat
on the throne of the Mandingo people for seventeen years,
he thought. My great ancestor, Sundiata, built the Mali Empire, but I have been a not unworthy successor. Under my
rule new kingdoms have bowed before the might of the army
of Mali. Our trade is rich and our fame has spread to the shores of
far-off seas. Mandingo children will praise my name in times to
come, and poets will sing of the glories of our empire. But I am
weary of conquest and government, of taxes and tribute, of all
worldly cares. I long to pray at the Temple of Abraham and to
stand before the sacred Black Stone.

Lost in reverie, the Emperor scarcely heard the soft footfall
of a servant who glided into the room. Humbly, the servant
leaned forward to knock his elbows on the ground and then
waited, head bowed, for Mansa Musa to give him leave to
speak. With a wave of his hand, the Emperor signified his
permission.

"Most noble master, the scholar for whom you sent has arrived.
He attends your pleasure."

"Send him in, send him in at once!" Mansa Musa paced
back and forth impatiently, breaking into speech the moment
the learned man entered the room.

"No, no, let us not waste time with idle ceremonies. I do not
wish to hear the greetings due an emperor, but to obtain your
advice as a pilgrim. Tell me, man of wisdom, which would be
the most auspicious day for me to begin my *hadj*?"

The scholar nodded his head thoughtfully as he pondered
the Emperor's question. After a few moments of silence, during
which the ruler stared at him eagerly, the professor spoke.

"You must wait, my lord, for a Saturday which falls on the twelfth day of the month. On that day and no other must you depart."

Now that the day of departure could be set, the city of Niani hummed with ceaseless activity. Washing their clothes in the river, the women of Niani chattered constantly of the preparations for the great event.

"Have you heard," said one woman as she beat the cotton garments on the stones at the river bank, "that a caravan arrived yesterday from Takedda? They say that the camels were so weary under the weight of the copper that some of them died of exhaustion while the load was being taken from their backs!"

"The mines of Takedda are many weeks' march from Niani. My brother is a camel driver and has seen the city with his own eyes. Caravans come there from far-off places that none of us will ever see—from Egypt, from the sands of Cyrenaica, from a mysterious place across the great water."

Scornfully, another woman interrupted. "Your brother and his stories, indeed! My uncle carries water to the Emperor's palace— I could really tell you tales, if I chose."

"Do tell us, oh, do!" cried the other women. Proud of being the center of attention, the speaker continued.

"Last week, my uncle says, the Emperor himself broke bread with a party of cannibals. Imagine!"

"I don't believe it," interjected another voice. "Why would our ruler do such honor to heathen savages?"

"Because, ignorant one, they possess a gold mine, and much gold is needed for the *hadj*. Oh, they are rich, those cannibals— wearing silken cloaks and covered with ornaments. My uncle vows that he heard something about them that will make your blood run cold." All the women shuddered deliciously. "Come closer, and I will tell you. One of the palace slaves told my uncle that the great Mansa gave the cannibals a hospitality gift of a young slave girl, a real beauty. Our King thought, no doubt, that she would please them with her singing and soft ways. Do you know what they did? They killed her and made a meal of her! Then they returned to our Emperor, their cruel faces smeared with her blood, and thanked him for his gift."

Several women cried out in protest. "I don't believe a word of it!" "Gossip and idle tales!" "You should be ashamed to repeat such talk."

Sulking, the storyteller turned back to her washing while the other women continued to chatter. "I myself know nothing of cannibals, but I have heard strange reports of the Wangara people in the far-off gold country," a wizened old crone commented. "No one knows where their gold mines are hidden, deep in their marshy forests. When the Emperor sends merchants to trade for Wangara gold, they cannot even find the Wangara people to bargain with them! Our merchants lay their goods in heaps on the river bank and then withdraw to their camp. Silently, when no one can see them, the Wangara creep out to examine the salt or beads or cloth left for them. Then they take what they want, leaving gold dust in exchange. Our merchants come back when all is quiet. They beat the drums and take the gold, never even seeing those with whom they traded."

"Either the Wangara are very timid," laughed another washerwoman, "or perhaps they do not know how to speak!" The women chuckled as they gathered up their clothes, and in a few moments all was quiet as their voices faded in the shimmering air and the little pools of muddied water dissolved in the gentle waves of the river's edge.

The streets of Niani bulged with the thousands of people who had assembled to accompany Mansa Musa on the *hadj*. The neighing of spirited horses mingled with cries of hawkers, the clanking of chain mail, the thud of camels' hooves. Odors of food cooking on open fires drifted through the air. It seemed that the city could scarcely contain the flood of activity which swirled within it.

In the cool stillness of his dressing chamber in the palace, Mansa Musa prepared for the final audience to be held for his court before the pilgrimage. His household slaves fluttered around him, bringing the brilliant garments befitting the ruler of a mighty domain. The Emperor stepped into his royal trousers, tight at the leg and billowing wide through the seat, trousers made of twenty widths of cloth. One slave adjusted the Mansa's red velvet tunic, another placed the royal golden skullcap on his brow, still another handed him his bow and hung the gold quiver on his back. In full regal array, the Mansa strode majestically from the room while his servants scraped the ground with their elbows as he passed.

In the courtyard, the waiting throng stood quietly, their eyes fixed on the empty platform under the great tree in the center. Suddenly the thin sound of plucked guitar strings, faint at first and then steadily louder, filled the air. Twanging their two-stringed gold and silver instruments, the Emperor's musicians marched into the courtyard. Behind them, his head held high, Mansa Musa walked, the musicians opening a path for him to mount the three steps of the silk-carpeted platform. As the Emperor seated himself on the ivory bench, the three hundred armed slaves who had followed him took their stations surrounding the platform. The chief officers of the army, seated in two semicircles below, saluted the Emperor, as did the principal cavalry officers seated beyond them.

The courtyard was filled with people in fine white cotton garments, wearing turbans attached under their chins. As proof of valor, certain warriors in the crowd wore gleaming gold bracelets. Others, with more valiant deeds to their credit, were adorned with gold collars; those with the greatest deeds of bravery displayed the golden ankle bracelets to which their daring entitled them. These officers wore the wide trousers which their Emperor had bestowed on them as a sign of honor; each successive feat was rewarded with wider trousers, though never as billowing as those of the sovereign himself.

A fanfare of trumpets and bugles and the wild beating of the drums announced the beginning of the audience. The spectacle for which the court had assembled unrolled in a tapestry of glittering color and ceremony. Thirty young men, their white skullcaps and scarlet tunics blazing in the sunlight, kept up a steady drumbeat while another group of youths flipped their lithe bodies in a series of cartwheels and handsprings. Still others displayed their swordsmanship for the Emperor's pleasure, their blades gleaming with each thrust and parry, the golden scabbards at their side twinkling in the brilliant sunshine as they moved.

When the youths had retired, all was still. But the pageant had only begun, for the captain of the Emperor's guard appeared, followed by a procession of his four wives and their hundred slave girls. The thin robes of the women fluttered about their ankles in the gentle breeze, and the gold and silver bands in their hair shone softly. Swinging a crystal mace, the captain made obeisance to the Emperor and then began a chant in praise of his noble deeds.

"Great is our ruler, mighty are his accomplishments. The people of Kabara, Zagha, Tichit, Walata, Tadmekket, Araouan and Agades all humble themselves before him. From the infinite ocean to the darkling forest, from the burning sands to the tender grassland, the name of Mansa Musa resounds in glory. Allah the Merciful rains blessings on him and on his children, the Mandingo people!" As the captain chanted, the crowd in the courtyard echoed his words softly. When he had at last finished, there was a quick motion of the Emperor's hand, and in an instant a bag of gold was placed before the singer.

Next came a cortege of fantastic feathered figures, each with a wooden head and bright-red beak, like giant thrushes. These were the poets of the court, come to recite their verses so that the shining past and present glory of Mali could be re-created for each listener. When the last and most beautiful of the poems had been spoken, the chief poet moved solemnly forward. Mounting the third step of the platform, he knelt and laid his head in the Emperor's lap. Then he rose and, bending beneath the arch of carved tusks over the ivory throne, put his head first on Mansa Musa's right shoulder and then on his left. The ritual completed, the chief poet turned and led the other poets from the courtyard while the soft twanging of many bowstrings accompanied their departing footsteps.

The crowd fell silent as a fanfare of trumpets announced that the Emperor was about to speak.

"People of Mali, I bid you farewell on the eve of a great undertaking. Tomorrow I leave to fulfill my dearest wish, to kneel in the holy places of our faith and lift my prayers to Allah the Merciful. The journey will be long and, once we have left the safe confines of our Empire, dangerous. But do not fear for me or those who accompany me, for Allah has spoken through the lips of a learned man to assure our safe return.

"Let there be peace and prosperity in Mali during my absence. My son Maghan will rule in my place. To him, all obedience must be given. Let no man forget his duty to the Emperor while I am gone, for each will be dealt with on his merits when I return. My tax collectors will continue to take the Emperor's just share of your sales of crops and livestock and of the value of the goods you bring into the kingdom or sell in foreign lands. The army of Mali will protect you, as it has ever done, and throughout the length and breadth of our Empire you will find safe passage, as always, for your trade and commerce.

"Follow the teachings of the Prophet, may his name be blessed, and may Allah hear your every prayer. Farewell."

That evening, dressed in the clean white garments that they always wore on Friday, the most important day of their faith, the people of Niani joined in their congregations for prayer. Kneeling on their woven palm-leaf prayer mats, the worshipers silently repeated the words of the Fatiha, the opening chapter of the Koran. When the services drew to a close and the imam called out, "Peace be on you and the blessings of Allah," each white-robed figure echoed the call in his heart: "Peace be on you, O Emperor, and the blessings of Allah."

The first faint streaks of dawn glowed in the east the next morning as the vast assemblage gathered on the outskirts of Niani began to stir. As the sun rose, the call to prayer rang through the camp: "Allah is great, Allah is great, Allah is great, Allah is great. . . . I bear witness that Mohammed is the messenger of Allah. . . . come to prayer, come to prayer, come to salvation. . . ." A multitude of faces turned toward Mecca; a multitude of bodies prostrated themselves in devotion. With the words of the final prayer resounding through the motionless air, the immense caravan began to move. "In the name of Allah, who sustains and provides for us and blesses all righteous action with beneficent reward." The pilgrimage had begun.

How many thousands accompanied Mansa Musa on his *hadj*? There are no exact figures, but scholars believe that perhaps as many as 60,000 people made the journey. In advance of the Emperor went 500 slaves, each carrying a staff of gold weighing five or six pounds. Following him, a hundred camels plodded across the desert sands, each bearing some 300 pounds of gold dust. Scores of other camels carried the enormous quantities of food, supplies and clothing needed for the months of travel that lay ahead.

Riding his white Arab steed, the Mansa could see his caravan stretching endlessly both before and behind him. A sly smile played about the Emperor's lips as he thought of the many chieftains whom he had honored by requesting their presence on the *hadj*—an honor indeed, but one whose more subtle purpose was to prevent these same chiefs from carrying out any power-hungry dreams they might have of chopping away at the Empire of Mali during Musa's absence. Then his thoughts turned to the other invited members of the caravan—the noblemen, the doctors, the professors, the jurists, the friends and relatives who, like himself, were about to see the holy places of Islam. Even the soldiers, the porters, the drivers, the artisans, the slaves and servants who ministered to the daily needs of each noble traveler, would share the glorious opportunity. I have done much for Mali, the Emperor thought; my armies have plucked new territories as a man plucks the ripe melon from the vine; my merchants have swelled the coffers of the kingdom with riches from every part of the world; any man may travel from Niani to Takedda, from Koumbi to Taghaza, secure in the knowledge that no bandit will seize his goods, no brigand threaten his life. But nothing have I done that can compare with this pilgrimage, this holy journey in praise of Allah, the Most Gracious. All thanks to God, who has made possible this *hadj*!

Slowly, majestically, the caravan proceeded northward toward Walata, nearly a month's march away. The fertile fields surrounding Niani, filled with various beans, onions, garlic, eggplant, cabbage, gourds, fruit and nut trees, gave way to short, dry, brown grasses, with only an occasional village dotted here and there. Wandering herdsmen, driving their flocks of sheep and goats before them, stopped to stare in open-mouthed astonishment as the enormous procession flowed past them. When the caravan halted for the night, timid village women edged their way out of their clustered clay houses, bearing half-calabashes full of pounded millet mixed with honey and milk, squawking chickens or mashed beans. Servants bargained busily for these additions to the provisions they had brought with them, paying the villagers for the extra supplies with cowrie shells or pieces of salt or glass ornaments. Sometimes the caravan halted as it passed an ancient baobab tree, its huge hollow trunk filled with collected rainwater, which was promptly used to replenish the empty waterskins of those lucky enough to reach the tree first.

Thus the immense procession moved slowly forward, edging its way step by step to Walata, on to Tuat and into the vast expanses of the Sahara Desert. The days followed one another in unending monotony. The brilliant desert sun beat fiercely down on the throng of travelers, and the chill desert night winds pierced their bones. Arrival at an oasis, with its irrigation canals carefully tended by slaves belonging to Arab or Tuareg masters, provided an occasional respite. The welcome green of the date palms soothed the eye, as the taste of newly picked fruits and vegetables or the chill of freshly drawn water invigorated the palate.

One night on the journey, it is told, Mansa Musa's splendid tent had been readied as usual so that he and his wife, Inari Konte, could rest comfortably. Weary of the long day's ride on his Arab stallion, the Emperor fell quickly asleep, only to be awakened in a short while by his wife's restless tossing in her bed.

"Why are you wakeful?" he inquired tenderly.

Her black eyes glowed in the faint candlelight flickering in the tent. "I long for our beautiful river to bathe in," she replied "I am weary, and my body is veiled with the grime of travel. How I long to splash about and swim carefree in the river! You are a great Emperor. Can you command a river to course through the desert sands?"

The Mansa leapt from his bed to summon Farba, the chief of his train of slaves. As he entered the tent, Farba whipped off his tunic and wrapped it around himself, then bowed low while he beat his chest. Slipping to his knees after this ritual greeting, Farba awaited his master's command.

"O Farba, since we have been married, my wife has never asked for anything outside my power to give, anything which I could not accomplish. But tonight she has asked me to make the river spring from the nothingness of the desert. Only God can do such a thing. I am powerless!"

Beating his chest, Farba exclaimed, "May Allah the All-Merciful accomplish your wish!" Then he withdrew from the Emperor's presence, while in the dark stillness Inari Konte moaned softly in her discomfort.

Back at his own camp, Farba called the slaves together and issued his instructions. Each man was to take a hoe and dig out the earth along a thousand-foot line that Farba would mark. As the slaves worked, a wall of earth was thrown up, reaching

three times the height of a man. Next the trench was lined
with gravel and packed with sand for its entire length. On top
were placed blocks of wood, which were then rubbed with the
oil of kharite nuts. One touch of a flaming torch, and the melting
oil filled in every crevice to form a smooth channel. Then the
slaves were sent for water, and in a few moments the huge canal
was filled with gently rolling waves. A miniature river had sprung
from the desert!

Back at the Emperor's tent, Farba found the royal couple
sleepless because of the eddying smoke and the crackle of the
flames. Breathlessly, he bowed. "Sire, Allah has come to your
aid and dispelled your cares. Where is Inari? Let her come,
since God has empowered you to create the river which she
desired."

The sun was just beginning to rise as the princess, looking
dazed, mounted her mule to go to the river which had miracu-
lously appeared. Her 500 women followed silently behind—but
the silence was shattered by the shrieks of joy and astonishment
of the laughing, unbelieving women as they plunged into the
water. Mansa Musa's princess had been granted her wish.

After many months, the great caravan drew near Cairo. There
the travelers would rest, restock their provisions in the city's
busy bazaars, and make merry before continuing on to Mecca.
As the caravan approached the outskirts of Cairo, a richly clad
Egyptian came galloping toward the Mandingo Emperor, his
sturdy brown Arab stallion tossing its head to scatter the white
foam from its panting mouth.

"The noble Sultan of Egypt, El-Malik en-Nasir, sends you
greetings, great king. I am Emir Abu-l-Abbas Ahmed ben Abi,
and I bid you welcome to our country in the name of the Sultan.
He prays that the blessings of Allah may be showered upon you,
and awaits your presence in his palace."

Mansa Musa stared proudly at the messenger. Although he
knew Arabic, he did not wish to speak in a foreign tongue. He

signaled for an interpreter and, when the translation had been completed, replied to Abu in a rapid flow of the language of Mali. "I thank your Sultan and return his greeting. But I have crossed the desert only to make a pilgrimage to the holy places of our Faith, not for anything else. It is my wish only to follow the footsteps of the Prophet, may peace be with him, and not to commingle worldly acts with my *hadj*."

Emir Abu gaped at the black sovereign who so cavalierly turned aside the request of the Sultan of Egypt. How could he return to the imperial household with this refusal? Pleading, Abu urged the Mansa to reconsider; his own honor would be ground into the dust if the Emperor did not change his mind. At length, Mansa Musa sighed impatiently, saying that he would attend the Sultan at his palace after a suitable period of rest and refreshment. With that, curtly ignoring the emir's urging to comply more promptly with the Sultan's request, the Emperor wheeled his horse about to indicate, unmistakably, that the conversation had terminated.

Upon entering Cairo, Mansa Musa proceeded directly to the suburb of Birket-el-Habech. A wealthy merchant of Alexandria, Siradj-ed-Din, had offered his elegant and spacious country home for the Emperor's use. Luxuriating in these pleasant surroundings after the weary months in the desert, the Mansa was in no hurry to seek out the Sultan and pay him compliments. Far better for a time to rest, bathe, pray and lie in the cool shade of a darkened room while musicians plucked lightly at their guitars and little red-throated chaffinches whistled gaily in the courtyard outside.

When the Mansa was finally ready for his audience with the Sultan, his servants robed him in his richest attire. We will meet as equals, the Emperor thought; I will never kiss the ground beneath the Sultan's feet, as is the custom here in Egypt. As the Mansa of Mali and his attendants, brilliant in gold and red, entered the audience chamber, the onlookers gasped at the splendid sight. Mansa Musa approached the Sultan with his head held high and his eyes locked with those of the Egyptian ruler. The crowd waited tensely while the Emperor stood, making no move to kneel before the Sultan. "He must kiss the earth"—the words flew back and forth across the room as the Egyptian courtiers stared at one another in disbelief.

"I kneel to no man," said the Mansa. "The rulers of Mali are the brothers of the rulers of Egypt, not their servants." Gravely, the Sultan stared back at Mansa Musa. The courtiers waited tensely, murmuring, "Who is this arrogant king from the Bilad-es-Sudan, the Land of the Blacks?" Suddenly, the ranks of the Emperor's attendants parted, as a scholar pushed his way forward to whisper urgently into Musa's ear. A broad smile broke across the Mansa's face, and he spoke again. "There is One to Whom I will bow. I will prostrate myself before Allah, Who created everyone and brought me into this world." So saying, he knelt and put his forehead to the ground.

Diplomacy had triumphed. The crisis over, Musa advanced toward the Sultan, who immediately arose to greet his guest with a warm, fraternal embrace. Then the Egyptian ruler invited the Emperor of Mali to sit next to him on the throne, where the two sovereigns held a long and intimate conversation while the dancers and musicians of the court performed for their pleasure.

One topic especially interested the Egyptian: the source of the enormous quantity of gold possessed by the Emperor of Mali. Mansa Musa may well have told the Sultan one of his favorite stories—that in a remote region of his empire, gold grew from the ground and was plucked like grain by the local inhabitants. But the people of the gold country had a strange power over the plants, the Emperor added smilingly, so that the gold plants could never be captured. Any attempt to invade the region caused the plants to stop growing. Only the people of the gold land knew how to cultivate the plants, and although they paid tribute to the Emperor, he knew that any effort to conquer them would mean the end of the golden harvest. The Sultan nodded at the tale, but understood its import—let no one hope to find the source of Mali's gold.

So pleased was El-Malik en-Nasir with his royal guest that he ordered a vast array of gifts to be sent to Mansa Musa upon his departure from the palace. Magnificent garments were presented to the Emperor, as well as clothing of all descriptions for his entourage. A train of spirited Arabian horses awaited the Emperor and his principal officers. Abundant foodstuffs, too, were presented. Gifts from the royal Egyptian palace to the Emperor of Mali came in an unceasing flow during the entire time that the caravan remained in Cairo.

Wherever he had passed on his way to Egypt, Mansa Musa had scattered alms. Each city and each village along the route of the pilgrimage had received the charity that the Moslem faith requires of its followers. Now the golden flood of alms distributed by the devout and generous Emperor reached its peak. Throughout Cairo the Mansa showered gold on every courtier, every officer and every official with whom he came in contact. Cairo shimmered in a golden haze; never had there been such an immense supply of the precious metal. The price of gold began to fall sharply, and even twelve years later the Arab chronicler al-Omari, visiting the city, found to his dismay that the gold market remained depressed.

The merchants and shopkeepers of Cairo, however, were far from dismayed by the wealth and free-spending habits of Mansa Musa and his retinue. The bazaars displayed their finest merchandise to attract the visitors, who wandered from street to street sampling the bewildering array of wares. There were heady perfumes of civet, amber and musk; on another street, the drapery shops displayed silks and damasks, lush velvets and supple cloth of gold imported from Italy, fine linens and tightly woven cottons. Nearby, on the street of the Persian merchants, the gleam of precious stones mingled with the fragrance of exotic spices. Cookshops enticed the visitor with cheeses, flasks of fruit drinks, hearty pancakes fried in oil, delicately flavored sweetmeats and piles of eggs. There were heaps of pomegranates and quinces from Syria, as well as the glowing colors of cloth of India.

Despite the high prices, the travelers bought freely of the seemingly limitless supply of goods in Cairo's shops. No matter that they might pay five dinars for a shirt that everyone knew was worth only one; the gold of Mansa Musa was enough to meet every demand. Even the street jugglers' little trained birds grew rich; if one gave the bird a coin, it would fly to a box and bring a scroll with one's fortune on it.

The varied sights of Cairo delighted the visitors. Wandering through the Garden, a pleasure park and promenade on the banks of the Nile, they could gaze dreamily at the numerous boats gliding by on their way to Upper Egypt or downstream to Alexandria and Damietta. They could worship at the many mosques, making sure to attend the important Friday services at the gorgeous Mosque of 'Amr. They could visit the hospital built by Sultan Qalá'-ún some forty years earlier, where every known medicine or medical appliance could be bought. Or they could watch the merry street festivals, when the bazaars were decorated with glittering ornaments and silken fabrics and wandering musicians and jugglers performed for the passing crowds.

The pleasures and luxuries of Cairo, however, were not the goal of Mansa Musa's pilgrimage. Impatiently he prepared for the remainder of the journey, and as soon as all was in readiness, he ordered that the caravan set out for Mecca. Sultan El-Malik en-Nasir, meanwhile, had not neglected to provide for the comfort and safety of the travelers. His messengers had carried written orders that all along the route were to recognize the authority of Mansa Musa, pay him respect and minister to his needs. Feeding stations for the camels and horses were established, and as a parting gesture, the Sultan presented Mansa Musa with a gift of money and a variety of provisions, as well as camels complete with saddle and harness for the Emperor's retainers. Small wonder that when the Mandingo ruler returned from the holy cities, he bore with him rich quantities of gifts for the Sultan.

Nearing Mecca, the caravan paused to make ready for the holy city. In his tent, Mansa Musa removed his rich clothing to put on the *ihram*, the simple garment which all pilgrims wear so that each may appear without distinction of wealth or position. He draped the two lengths of plain white cloth over his body and fastened them, leaving his head, hands, ankles and feet uncovered, as well as his right shoulder and arm. Now the mighty Emperor, all signs of rank effaced, could worship Allah in pureness of heart and deep devotion. He was no longer the Mansa, but only a humble and devout child of God. Like the Prophet, he took the vows of the pilgrimage: to abstain from sin and evil thoughts and to do no harm to any living creature.

The sight of Mecca seemed to Mansa Musa almost miraculous, as though a dream had suddenly taken on form and substance. He felt himself transported to the days when Abraham had made the first pilgrimage to Mecca and with his son Ishmael had built the House of God, the Kaaba. His heart beating heavily, the pilgrim Musa approached the enclosure of the sacred house and burst into prayer.

Then Musa performed the ritual circuit of the Kaaba, starting at the southeast corner in which stands the Black Stone of Adam. Seven times he circled the House of God, and then entered the plain stone building, lighted by dimly flickering candles, in order to kiss the Black Stone as Mohammed had done before him. He was oblivious of the other pilgrims performing the same devotions, aware only of his own sense of oneness with God.

The days that followed in Mecca were a continuing series of religious ceremonies. In memory of the agonized search for water of Ishmael's mother, Hagar, the pilgrim ran seven times between Safa and Marwah, two small hills near the Kaaba in the middle of Mecca. Then he drank from the Zam Zam, the spring which God had revealed to Hagar to end her frantic quest. At another time, he rode out of Mecca and onto the Plain of Arafat to attend the services held there. He knelt in prayer at the heap of boulders where Adam had begged God's mercy, and later he threw rocks at the great stone column which symbolized the evil spirit that had tempted Abraham. At Muzdalifah, where Abraham had heard God's command to offer his son in sacrifice, the pilgrim worshiped Allah. And at Mina Gorge, where Abraham had killed the ram, Mansa Musa too offered a ram in sacrifice.

In the hours that were not spent in religious devotions, the Emperor talked with the many holy and educated men of Mecca. He made the acquaintance of the Granada-born Arab poet and architect Abu-Ishaq Ibrahim-es-Saheli, and the two men found one another so compatible that es-Saheli agreed to accompany Mansa Musa back to Mali.

Most especially, the Emperor wished to have several descendants of the Prophet return home with him. "I ask you," he said to the Sheikh of Mecca, "to give me three or four sharifs to take back to my kingdom. The sight of such personages of the Prophet's holy line, may Allah's blessings fall upon him, will be a source of benediction to those who dwell in Mali."

"It is impossible," replied the Sheikh. "Despite my wish to do you every honor, I cannot disregard the noble blood of the sharifs. Nor can I risk their falling into the hands of infidels, for I am told that many pagans still inhabit your Empire. The descendants of Fatima, daughter of the Prophet, may God give him peace, might disappear or be lost in the vast stretches of Mali. No, no, it cannot be done."

Mansa Musa regarded the Sheikh thoughtfully. "It is true that there are those in my kingdom who do not know the true Faith. There are indeed tribes who pay me allegiance but still worship their pagan gods. Yet it is also true that throughout the length and breadth of Mali all persons are secure and can move about without fear of attack. If you would give me the sharifs, I could guarantee their absolute safety. No danger would come near them under my care."

The Sheikh, perhaps a little irritated by the Emperor's persistence, exploded into speech. "No, no, I will not do it! I will give no orders on this matter!" Then suddenly his face relaxed. "This is what I will do, O Emperor. I will not demand it of the sharifs, but I will not forbid it. Let those who wish it make the choice to follow you. As for me, I take no responsibility. It is up to the sharifs themselves."

Immediately the Mansa called a herald to him. "Let it be announced in the mosque that 1,000 mithqals of gold will be paid at once to any of the Prophet's line, may Allah rain blessings on him, who wish to follow me to my country. Honor and riches to those who heed my call!" To Mansa Musa's joy, four Qureishites, descendants of Hashim, the great grandfather of Mohammed, responded to the invitation and returned to Mali with the caravan.

The Emperor and his retinue found themselves charmed by the people of Mecca, elegantly clad in snowy-white garments, their dark eyes outlined in kohl, their skins sweet with perfume. These gracious people seemed particularly kind to strangers and to the poor. Meccans taking their bread back home from the public bakehouses gladly distributed a share to the beggars who followed them. At the bazaar, where the townsmen came to buy foodstuffs, orphan children sat waiting with baskets to carry the purchases. Each child, for a small sum of money, would put cereals into one basket and meat and vegetables into another, and scurry off to deliver his burden at the buyer's home. Never did the children abuse the confidence placed in them; each basket arrived at its destination intact. Trust, open-heartedness, courtesy, cleanliness—all of these marked the people of the holy city.

As the days of prayer, religious devotions, and conversations with learned men sped by, the Emperor found himself more and more attracted to the holy and scholarly life he was leading.

Now I must return to Mali, he thought, but I know how I wish to spend the remainder of my days. When I am back home, I shall make all the required plans for the future security of Mali, but I will not remain there. I shall yield the throne to my son and come back to Mecca, where I can live out my earthly time in meditation and piety. This is my true desire.

Eager to forward his plan of abdication, Mansa Musa decided to leave the holy city at once. Having scattered gifts lavishly in Mecca as he had in Cairo, the Emperor proceeded northward to Medina. With reverence he approached the Mosque of the Apostle, where Mohammed lies buried, his face toward Mecca. As Musa halted to pray at the Gate of Peace, the wailing voices of the muezzins floated down from the five tall, square minarets of the mosque: "Allah is Great . . . come to Prayer, come to Salvation. . . ." Mansa Musa entered the mosque and prostrated himself at the Prophet's grave, murmuring, "Peace be upon thee, O Apostle. We witness that thou hast endeavored in God's way until God glorified His religion and perfected it." The Emperor prayed long and silently at Mohammed's tomb, invoking the peace of Allah not only on the Prophet but on Abu Bakr and Umar, the first two caliphs, who lie buried next to him. Then the sovereign moved to touch the fragment of the palm trunk against which Mohammed had stood when he preached. "I praise Thee, O God," he murmured, "for having allowed me to reach the former dwelling and glorious sanctuaries of Thy holy Prophet."

During his stay in Medina, Mansa Musa visited the many sites where Mohammed had received revelations, praying devoutly at each sacred spot. He made his devotions at Quba Mosque, the first mosque of Islam, outside the city. But often at night he turned back to the Mosque of the Apostle. There, in the bizarre shadows cast by the candles they had lighted, the pilgrims sat in large circles in the courtyard, reciting the Koran from volumes set on rests in front of them. The sound of litanies, intoned softly by the many devout voices, rose and fell in a rhythmic chant. Mansa Musa, his spirit swelling with happiness, knew himself to be fully at peace.

But the days of the *hadj* were drawing to a close. The final impetus to start the long homeward journey came when the Emperor received word by messenger that his army was engaged in an active campaign against the neighboring kingdom of Songhai. The moment had come to set off again for Cairo. Then would come the interminable march across the desert.

When the caravan re-entered Cairo and began to reprovision for the remaining journey, the Emperor discovered, somewhat to his embarrassment, that his seemingly inexhaustible supply of gold was in fact at the point of exhaustion. He was amused by the eagerness with which the Egyptian merchants flocked to offer him loans; clearly his wealth had so impressed Cairo that there were no limits to his credit. Borrowing a large sum from his former host, Siradj-ed-Din, a loan later to be repaid at the princely rate of 1000 dinars for each 300 lent, Mansa Musa quickly arranged for the caravan to continue. Although he wished to return to Mecca as soon as possible, the desire to see Mali again now seized his spirit. The trip across the Sahara seemed endless to him, and he drove forward with ever-increasing impatience.

For many years before the *hadj*, Mansa Musa had gloried in his great success in war. In his breast the old martial fervor once more leaped high when he heard the good news which reached him during the desert crossing. An exhausted herald galloped into camp, gasping that Sagamandia, one of the Mandingo generals, had captured the prosperous city of Gao. The thriving agriculture and commerce of the Songhai empire, of which Gao was the chief city, would be added to the wealth and power of Mali. Pridefully, Mansa Musa announced to es-Saheli, who had become one of his closest companions, that he would stop at Gao before reaching Mali. There he would personally receive the submission of Dia Assibai, ruler of Songhai.

Mansa Musa's triumphal entry into Gao in 1325 meant a significant expansion of the Empire of Mali. The busy bazaars of the city were filled with merchandise from distant lands, brought by caravans from Ghana, Tunis, Iberia, Cyrenaica and

Egypt. The bustling trade of the city impressed the Emperor, but he was shocked by the fact that the mosque there was nothing but a straw-roofed mud hut. After the glorious mosques of Cairo and the holy cities, the simple, ordinary structure at Gao seemed unthinkably humble. Calling es-Saheli to him, the Mansa asked his friend to take charge of building a great mosque to the never-ending glory of God. When the new mosque was completed, the muezzin could stand high on its pyramidal minaret to send his wailing call to prayer far and wide.

When he left Gao, Mansa Musa was accompanied by two hostages, Ali Kolen and Sulaiman Nar, the two sons of Dia Assibai. Shrewd as ever in matters of state, the Emperor had guaranteed that the Songhai ruler would pay tribute and follow the commands of his new liege lord.

Pressing onward, the Mansa followed the winding course of the Niger River to Timbuktu. As the caravan moved toward the city, hippopotamuses lifted their sluggish heads from the cool water to peer myopically at the travelers. Villagers emerged from their small conical mud houses to gape at the vast entourage. Exhausted as they were, the members of the caravan laughed and joked together, oblivious of whatever sights might otherwise have attracted their glance. The thought of home was effacing the memories of the journey, and it was only the Emperor's decision to stop and annex the city of Timbuktu that enforced a sudden brief halt in the headlong rush toward Niani.

The lack of a proper mosque at Timbuktu, as at Gao, prompted Mansa Musa to ask es-Saheli to undertake the building there of a mosque as well as a new royal palace. Later travelers were astonished by the beautiful square palace with its airy porch and soaring cupola, the plaster walls brilliantly decorated with intricate arabesques in flaming colors. But Mansa Musa, eager to be on his way, had no thought of waiting to see his order carried out. He appointed a governor for the newly conquered city and turned his attention to the last lap of the incredible journey, some 10,000 miles in all. Casting aside the exhausted mounts of his personal retinue, the Emperor ordered a fleet of barges to be assembled in the wide expanse of the Niger River. The ruler, his wives, the Qureishites and their families, all garbed in silks and brocades, boarded the vessels. The heavily loaded barges moved slowly upstream, pennants flying, as Niani prepared to receive its Emperor.

The boom of drums, the merry twang of guitars and the loud call of horn trumpets announced the return of Mansa Musa to his capital. His head shaded from the sun by a horseman carrying a broad parasol surmounted by a flag, the Emperor rode into the city which he had not seen for over a year. Joyfully he greeted his son Maghan, who had ruled in his place during the long absence, and devoutly he gave his thanks to Allah for the successful *hadj*. Rejoicing and festivals of welcome filled Niani, and the entire city gave way to feasting and celebration.

In the seven years that followed, the Mansa was to think often and longingly of his desire to lead a life of contemplation in Mecca. Now that affairs of government again claimed his attention, it seemed impossible to abdicate and leave the kingdom. The Empire, unlike the nations of today, was not a tightly knit and cohesive country. It was a loose confederation, whose subject provinces had to be supervised carefully. If the powerful army of Mali was not present to enforce the Emperor's decrees, local chieftains or vassal rulers were ever ready to slip out of control, refusing to pay the allotted tribute. Only by force of personal strength, dedication to the Empire's welfare and strong administrative ability could Mali be held secure and unified. The hope of leaving the kingdom under the rule of his son Maghan glimmered fitfully in the Emperor's heart and then died out. He sadly came to recognize the weakness and lack of self-discipline in his heir, and he feared for Mali's safety on the inevitable day when his death would bring Maghan to the throne. Nor was this fear exaggerated, for the four years during which Maghan ruled after Mansa Musa's death in 1332 marked the beginning of the decline of the great Empire of Mali.

Maghan's reign furnished a portent of the coming Empire of

Songhai, which was to rise and replace Mali as the major power of the western Sudan. The two hostages whom Mansa Musa had seized at Gao on his triumphal return from the pilgrimage slipped through Maghan's fingers. Back at Gao, Ali Kolen and Sulaiman Nar laid the foundation of the future aggrandizement of Songhai. Over the course of almost two hundred years, culminating in the powerful and expansionist rule of Askia Mohammed, Songhai eroded the fading strength of Mali. Slowly the great empire of the Mandingo people decayed and vanished, leaving only the dimming memory of its days of glory.

During the twenty-five-year reign of Mansa Musa, the fame of Mali had spread throughout the Western world. European kings envied his wealth and power; sultans from Fez to Egypt and Arabia sought his friendship and thrived on trade with his prosperous Empire. Scholars and jurists flocked to the great cities of Mali, and merchants crossed the vast kingdom confident of the safe passage of their teeming caravans. Like other great civilizations before and since, Mali's grandeur swelled and faded, perhaps to rise again as the spirit of his glory stirs today in the descendants of the magnificent Mansa Musa.

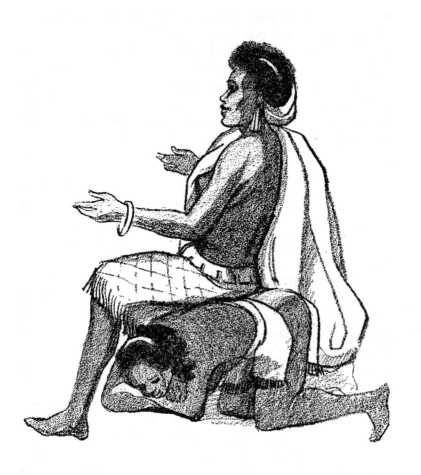

QUEEN NZINGA

IN the memory of everyone present, this was the most brilliant assemblage that had ever been gathered in the audience room of the Governor of Angola. Despite the stifling heat, all the high officials and magistrates of Luanda were there in full regalia—velveteen pantaloons and doublets, long hose and high ruffs constricting their necks like white, frilled snakes. Officers of the Portuguese army moved through the crowd carrying their gleaming, beplumed helmets, their ceremonial swords clanking at their sides. They were rough, bearded men with skins cured like leather in the merciless African sun.

The prosperous businessmen of this humid port city had been requested to attend, and they had left their shops and offices and slave blocks to accommodate the new governor, João Corrêa de Souza. Some had brought their wives, splendid in silks and jewels, their faces gleaming with sweat as they carefully measured each breath against the cruel pressure of their iron corset stays.

Dark-cassocked priests chatted easily with friends and parishioners, but the handful of Jesuits stood off to one side, somberly fingering their rosary beads. Along the fringes of the crowd the "good" native chiefs (Sobas) stood proudly erect, black hair plaited, teeth filed to points, freshly oiled tribal scars glistening, arms covered with bracelets of leather and copper wire. Every few feet throughout the audience chamber were stationed young slave boys bestirring the stagnant air with feathery green palm fronds.

Suddenly the doors flew open, and the soldiers on duty pushed back the crowd to clear an aisle. A solid phalanx of brightly clad Mbundu women came shuffling slowly forward, separating into two rows at the dais. As the escort moved back, a tall, handsome woman was left standing alone in the hushed hall. She appeared to be in her late twenties, although she was, in that year of 1622, forty years old. Her skirt hung in graceful folds of red and yellow native-spun cloth richly encrusted with cowrie shells. Over her breasts was draped a mantle of bright blue fastened with gleaming copper rings.

Her haughty gaze took in the situation quickly—there was but one chair, and it was carved with the seal of the Royal Governor.

In front of the Viceroy's chair was spread a magnificent carpet with two red velvet cushions embroidered in gold, obviously meant for her. For a brief moment displeasure clouded the woman's face, but with a sharp clap she beckoned one of her slaves. The girl went down on the rug on all fours. Her mistress imperiously seated herself on the back of the servant and awaited calmly the arrival of the Governor. A proud people themselves, the Portuguese smiled at each other and nodded their heads in approval of the African woman's spirit and dignity.

When Corrêa de Souza entered, he raised an eyebrow over the alteration in his seating arrangements, but, inclining his head in a slight bow, he proceeded without taking official notice.

"In the name of our Sovereign Felipe IV, I welcome the Princess Nzinga. Your brother Mbandi, the King of Ndongo, did well to choose so worthy an ambassador. I hope you have found your residence in the Governor's palace suitable."

He sank into the ornate chair as the interpreter translated his greetings into Mbundu.

From her peculiar sofa Nzinga responded serenely. "I bring greetings for the Governor from my brother the Ngola [King] of Ndongo, and through you to your master in your faraway homeland."

While the ceremonial greetings continued, a buzz of conversation filled the room. "King of Ndongo, indeed!" a perspiring merchant muttered to his wife. "An empty title! We destroyed his capital at Mbaka three years ago. He's trapped on an island in the Kwanza River."

"Well, if he controls nothing in Angola anymore," his wife whispered back, "why do we have to get all powdered and perfumed to pay court to this black heathen?"

On the other side of the room a grizzled Portuguese captain exploded with a sharp elbow in the ribs of his companion. "You hear that! When Mendes de Vasconcellos was governor, he set up Ngola-Ari as King of Ndongo. At least you can deal with him. Why are we honoring an ambassador from Ngola-Mbandi? He's rotting, holed up on his little island, and his sister comes to Luanda like a conqueror. I don't understand what's going on."

After reviewing the bloody events of the past, the Governor came to the point of the meeting. "The aim of the Portuguese has always been to live in peace with the Mbundu, to trade so that we may both benefit and to bring the word of our Savior, Jesus Christ, so that your people may enter the Kingdom of Heaven. To these ends I offer Ngola-Mbandi a treaty of friendship on the condition that the Portuguese soldiers and traders he now holds prisoner on Ndangi Island are returned unharmed."

"My people, the Mbundu," replied Nzinga courteously, "also desire nothing more than to live in peace. We wish to go back to our villages and rebuild our houses.

"Our hearts are touched that the Portuguese long to see their countrymen held captive by my brother. Then perhaps the Governor can understand that we too wish to see our people returned unharmed—our mothers and fathers and husbands and wives and brothers and sisters and all our kinsmen taken by the *pombeiros* [slave traders]."

The crowd gasped at Nzinga's insolence. Did she indeed have the effrontery to equate the life of a Christian European with that of a black pagan? How naïve she was, how impractical! To return the poor captive Portuguese, her brother had only to put them on a raft and float them downstream to the fort at Massangano. But how did she expect slaves taken over the years to be returned? Most of them had been shipped across the Atlantic to the sugar plantations of Brazil. And what of those who had died en route or had perished from the rigors of life in the New World?

"We cannot undo the past," said Corrêa de Souza with genuine sorrow, "but as Viceroy of Felipe IV, I am prepared to guarantee the right of Ndongo to exist as an independent kingdom with Ngola-Mbandi on its throne."

There was a stir among the chieftains who understood Portuguese. Was the puppet Ngola-Ari to be abandoned?

When Nzinga understood the translation, she asked the Governor quietly, "And if Ndongo is recognized as an independent kingdom, what do the Portuguese demand in return?" Corrêa de Souza's face was wreathed in a victorious smile. "We can discuss the matter of an annual tribute at a later time."

Nzinga leaned forward suddenly on her improvised chair. Pointing a finger at the Governor, she scornfully asked, "Why should Ngola-Mbandi, whose father ruled Ndongo and whose ancestors hover over the land, pay tribute to anyone? If the Governor wishes to live in peace, then he has only to withdraw his soldiers from Mbaka. The Mbundu people do not need a treaty, a worthless scrap of paper, to reassure them that the Ndongo kingdom has the right to exist!"

She turned to the guard of honor which surrounded the Governor. "Ngola-Mbandi is protected by the spirits of our forefathers on Ndangi Island. And if your soldiers draw near, we will blacken the air with flights of poisoned arrows—like ravens carrying scorpions. Half your men will be food for the crocodiles, and those who escape the river will die of disease in the bush and the jungles. The Portuguese will never put a rope around the neck of Ngola-Mbandi. Tribute, oh Governor, can only be demanded of a conquered people!"

Ngola-Mbandi had done well to send his sister. An outstanding swordsman, Corrêa de Souza recognized in Nzinga an ambassador as quick with ideas as he was himself with the foils. For a long while they fenced back and forth with sharp words. Slowly the details of the agreement were whittled into shape: the Mbundu would return the captives on Ndangi Island and help the Portuguese round up fugitive slaves; the Portuguese would withdraw from Mbaka and other Mbundu towns they occupied and help Ngola-Mbandi expel the cannibal Jagas from the Kingdom of Ndongo; each would assist the other against their common enemies. Most important, the treaty would be signed by Corrêa de Souza and by Nzinga, not as overlord and vassal but on equal terms as representatives of their independent countries.

Surrounded by her shuffling ladies-in-waiting, Nzinga left the audience chamber with her head held high. Outside, her musicians jumped up from the shade of a tamarind and greeted her with whistles, drums and the rasping rhythm of the notched *ndamba*. As they watched the colorful party move noisily toward the Governor's palace, where Nzinga was an honored guest, the Portuguese expressed their amazement at the scene they had witnessed.

One of the magistrates said, "It seems supernatural to hear a woman brought up among savages and wild beasts speak and argue with such eloquence and fitness of language." Crossing themselves, the others nodded in agreement.

In the center of a group of soldiers, one voiced the emotions of the rest. "That half-naked woman and all her Mbundu should have been clapped in the dungeon. How many more of our good comrades must die of poisoned arrows and fever before our new Governor understands what goes on here in Angola?"

One of the priests who stood nearby responded with resignation. "God in his own good time will reveal his wisdom to the new Governor. For forty years we have worked to bring the blessings of civilization and the word of Our Lord to these heathen souls. In Portugal there are no fevers or poisoned spears or Jaga cannibals. Our new Governor will soon realize that people who give orders in Lisbon do not always comprehend the realities in Africa."

"Maybe he will also soon realize that the chieftains are not going to deliver their quota of slaves unless they're forced to. The only languages they understand are spoken by the whip and the musket."

The soldier and the priest would both have been astonished to learn how much Governor Corrêa de Souza did understand of the situation in Angola. He knew that the former governor, Luis Mendes de Vasconcellos, had arrived full of good intentions. He proposed friendship with the natives as a substitute for harsh repression, encouraged the church fathers to educate Africans and sought fair trade agreements. He denounced the traders and conquistadores, whose greed for profit and power had pushed aside royal decrees meant to help the Mbundu.

Yet when Ngola-Mbandi refused to pay tribute, Vasconcellos had ordered the destruction of the capital at Mbaka. When Ngola-Mbandi sued for peace but held Portuguese captives for insurance, Vasconcellos had ordered ninety-four chieftains executed en masse. The Portuguese then formed an alliance with the wild Jagas, who went into the bush like hunting dogs to track down the Mbundu. Slave traders moved in after them, devastating the Kingdom of Ndongo. Entire communities were wiped out, and once again the barracoons on the Luanda waterfront were full of slaves.

To meet each crisis, Governor Vasconcellos had found that he had to discard more of his earlier views. When he left Angola after four years, he was a very rich man, full of good advice for his successor: "It is only by severity and fear that we can hold our own against these indomitable heathens. . . ."

Corrêa de Souza knew that he had to try to right some of the wrongs. He was humane and religious, but he was also a practical man. The Portuguese could no longer afford the toll of their bravest and finest soldiers in the endless guerrilla war or from the terrible African diseases. The Portuguese puppet, Ngola-Ari, did not command the loyalty of the chieftains. Only by regaining the confidence of Ngola-Mbandi and supporting him as King of Ndongo could peace and profitable trade with the interior of Angola be re-established. Only then could the Portuguese milk the richness of Ndongo and the other territories which made up the Angolan colony. And always, like vultures circling over a dying animal, there were the Dutch men-of-war offshore and the Dutch traders active in the northern regions. Therefore, Portugal's future clearly depended on this morning's agreements with Ngola-Mbandi's ambassador. It was strange that the King had sent a woman. But she had proved to be quite a woman, he thought.

When Nzinga and Corrêa de Souza again met, their talk was not of such earthly things as soldiers, hostages and trade arrangements. The Governor had been greatly impressed by her intelligence and force of personality; he hoped to persuade Nzinga to convert to Christianity and then assist in saving the souls of other Africans. In 1482 Diego Cão had discovered Angola and erected a stone emblazoned with the royal coat of arms surmounted by a cross at the mouth of the River Zaire (Kongo). Would not he, the Governor of Angola 140 years later, do an equal service for the Lord Jesus Christ if he emblazoned His truth in Nzinga's heart?

For her part, Nzinga was eager to absorb all she could about the Europeans. Despite her haughty manner, she had been deeply impressed by her visit to Luanda—by the broad, clean-swept avenues lined with palm trees and acacias, by the spacious stone and brick houses roofed with red tiles, by the churches lifting their steeples toward Heaven, by the bustling market spilling over with all the good things in life. Her success as her brother's ambassador had fed her ambition, and she had quickly grasped that whatever she could learn from the Portuguese would be to her advantage. Therefore, she accepted without hesitation the Governor's invitation to remain in Luanda as his guest.

During that year of 1622, Nzinga spent much of her time taking religious instruction. The Jesuit fathers found her an eager and intelligent pupil whose inquiring mind and unique ideas pulled them into far-reaching discussions and lively arguments.

She particularly cherished visits from a prosperous Luanda merchant, Gaspar Alvares, who had given most of his fortune to the Church for the purpose of educating African children. Often on a Sunday morning he would accompany the Princess as she followed the procession of black children from the church to the courtyard of the mission school. She took pleasure in listening as they were publicly catechized and awarded prizes.

Alvares explained some of the difficulties in educating these children of household slaves. "The Mbundu language has never been written down, so that up to now children could not learn to read or write in their native language. Ordinary lessons have been conducted in Portuguese, but religious instruction has, of course, been in Latin."

But now, he told Nzinga, there was a new method of instruction called the alphabetical game, in which teachers and students in the primary grades acted out a living charade. As the numbers of Mbundu-speaking priests increased, lessons could be conducted in the African language. Alvares introduced Father Matthew Cardozo, superior of the Jesuit College, who had just completed a catechism and grammar in the Mbundu language. Nzinga offered some suggestions and encouraged him to complete another project, a Mbundu prayer book. To assist these forward steps, Nzinga told Father Cardozo: "When I return to the court of my brother, I shall persuade him to grant a tract of land in the interior for a mission school and to protect it with his royal favor."

While she was in Luanda, Nzinga painstakingly investigated the mechanics of the slave trade which had so devastated Angola. She knew only too well the dread process in the interior of the country. *Pombeiros*, themselves often slaves, would lead a train of a hundred or more bearers who carried woven palm squares, cotton cloth from Europe, blocks of clear salt from Ndemba, cowrie shells, glass beads, looking glasses, elephant tails and cheap brandy made from Brazilian sugar. For these treasured commodities, human beings were traded.

For a year or two the *pombeiros* would wander, paying native chiefs for enemies taken in raids or for others who were a burden to the tribe because of drought and famine. The *pombeiros* would also visit the chain of Portuguese forts in the interior and purchase prisoners of war from the soldiers. As their stock of goods diminished and their train of chained human beings increased, they headed back to the port of Luanda. There, too, were sent the annual tribute of young adult slaves paid by the chieftains as the price of Portuguese friendship.

Alvares took Nzinga to the barracoons on the waterfront where newly arrived slaves were housed. First they were sorted according to the state of their health. The sick were quarantined, the starving fattened up. Those who were waiting to be transported to Brazil were used as work gangs on the Bengo River farms.

The Princess and her friend moved toward a stir of activity along the docks. Slaves were being counted before loading. "There is a standard measurement," Alvares explained. "Able-bodied slaves fifteen to twenty-five years old count for one piece of goods. Those between the ages of eight to fifteen and twenty-five to thirty-five are counted as three for two pieces. Slaves under the age of eight or in the thirty-five to forty-five-year range pass as two bodies to one measure."

"What about infants at their mothers' breasts?" asked Nzinga, pointing to a child clinging to a forlorn woman.

"They follow the mother without counting. A bonus for the owners if the child lives."

"And older people past forty-five?"

"They are given a value by expert assessors, according to their condition."

Suddenly a group of priests appeared and stationed themselves near the ship's gangplank. As the uncomprehending captives were herded past them, the fathers swung containers of holy water. "Your name is Peter; your name is John; yours is Francis. . . ."

Each slave was prodded to put out his tongue, on which some salt was placed. Then the priest gave him a scrap of paper with his new name written on it.

On board a black interpreter addressed them. "With this baptism you are already children of God. You are going to the lands of the Portuguese across the sea to a place called Brazil, where you will learn more of the Faith. Do not think about where you came from because you are starting a new life. Go with a good will."

The priests on the dock made a last gesture of blessing, and guards began to push the slaves below deck. A great confusion ensued, and Nzinga heard the cries of the trampled. Some frightened people ran to the side and jumped overboard. Weighted with heavy chains, they sank immediately. Nzinga watched in fascination as others were clubbed into submission, and the hatches were finally battened down.

"They'll have to stay down there till the ship sails in the morning," Alvares said apologetically. "Some will suffocate, and the conditions are not too sanitary, but how else can we keep them from escaping?"

To Nzinga it seemed incredible that the small Portuguese caravel could carry its cargo of 600 slaves. She plied Alvares with questions about the future of her countrymen. The crossing took thirty-five to sixty days, he told her, depending on which Brazilian city was their destination. From there they were sold and distributed to sugar plantations and mines all over South America.

"But while aboard they get warm food twice a day," the merchant explained, "African beans and then maize with palm oil and salt. Sometimes a piece of dried fish is thrown in. During the day they usually get farina and water, and everyone gets two or three pieces of old cloth with which to cover himself." "The Portuguese treat their slaves much better than other countries," he added defensively.

"You are wise businessmen to attend to your merchandise," Nzinga commented gravely. "But why are slave ships called by your countrymen *tumbeiros* [*undertakers*]?"

"Well, the slaves are rather tightly packed to maximize profit, and most owners try to cut their expenses by hiring a crew of only ten or twelve Europeans to get the ship across the ocean. Because of the fear of mutiny or mass suicide, the slaves are seldom brought up on deck for fresh air and exercise, and then only in small groups. But our ship captains do try to keep disease down by washing the deck every other day with vinegar. Unfortunately, despite our precautions, about one quarter die en route—but you should see how the Dutch and the English treat their slaves."

Nzinga abruptly turned her attention to the men on the dock who still worked on the account book. Eager to change the subject, Alvares explained, "They are figuring out the share of this load which goes to the Crown. And the ship owners also have to pay an export tax on each body to the Governor."

"So the Governor gains riches as the number of slaves grows? Is that why the *pombeiros* stir up the tribes to war against each other? And the governors give orders to the soldiers to attack us because, they say, we have not carried out our treaties?" Alvares remained silent. "I must advise the Governor," Nzinga added cynically. "He will never get rich if he trusts the cannibal Jagas to hunt slaves. They eat more than they deliver."

During her stay in Luanda, Nzinga became particularly fond of a young lay priest, Jerome Sequiera, who had traveled extensively in the interior of Ndongo and the neighboring kingdom of Matamba.

Sometimes she ordered closed *palanquins* to carry them to the outskirts of the city, where they could stroll beyond the red sandstone cliffs among thin euphorbia trees and squat hollow baobabs. One day she lifted the curtain she had drawn around her personal life.

"My father was a great and brutal tyrant," she began. "He was dethroned and killed by his indignant subjects about five years ago. But he forged a mighty alliance to protect our people," she added triumphantly. "If the Kongo chieftains had not begun to fight among themselves, and if the Jagas had not defected for Portuguese promises of riches in slave hunting, your armies would still be dying cooped up in the fort at Massangano— and you would still be throwing away lives trying to reach the silver mines you imagined to be at Kambembe. The Portuguese told my father that there is a fever that rages in the blood of white men and that your medicine men need silver to cure it. Why could you never believe there is no silver at Kambembe?"

She also told Sequiera of the struggle for succession among the old Ngola's possible heirs. Finally, the fighting battalions installed their choice, Mbandi, an illegitimate son by a slave woman. The new Ngola, Nzinga's brother, washed away his insecurity with rivers of blood, killing everyone who could possibly offer a challenge to his supremacy.

Sequiera was emboldened to ask, "Does a husband await your return to Ndangi Island?"

"Many husbands," she said abruptly. "Why does the god of the Portuguese order only one man to one woman, and they may not take another as long as they both live?"

"It is the law of God," Sequiera replied. "Have you children?"

"A son."

"Where is he now?"

"He dwells with the Supreme Being. According to our laws, the son of the king's eldest sister succeeds to the throne. My brother, Ngola-Mbandi, feared his heir, and so he sent my son to live with his ancestors," she said quietly. The young man bowed his head and made the sign of the cross.

After that she said no more about her home or family. She told him all the old myths of creation and the legends of how hundreds of years before, the Mbundu, along with other Bantu tribes, had come down out of the center of Africa. Their Ngola knew the secret of working iron, and led by this "blacksmith king," they settled in the area between the Dande River in the north and the Kwanza in the south, from the coast to the Kwango River far inland.

He heard for the first time the old tales of the coming of the white men on ships with wings that shone in the sun. The Mbundu saw the caravels rise from the depths of the sea. The Africans knew that these men were from the Land of the Spirits, for their faces were pale like the death masks the witch doctors used at funerals. It was observed that these newcomers remained healthy as long as they stayed on board their ship, for "it was their natural place," but when they came ashore, they grew yellow with the fever, and some swelled up, and some had their bones turn to water, and some spat blood and heaved black vomit. "Thus did our Mbundu ancestors try to protect their people by making the newcomers sick.

But no matter how many died, more kept coming. The white men have brought us nothing but wars and misery."

"You must not judge all of Portugal by those you see in Angola," Sequiera said sadly. "Many of Luanda's first citizens are descended from, or are themselves, deported criminals. As for the Army officers, they are almost all noblemen's younger sons whose eldest brothers will inherit the family title and lands and for whom Africa is a chance to gain glory and fortune. Even government officials will risk sickness and death for a few years to fatten their pocketbooks here."

"But the white men have also brought you many good things," he reminded her. "New products to grow. Better ways to farm. Education. The True Cross of Our Lord. Most Portuguese sincerely see themselves as spiritually elevated people bearing God's banner to the pagan. I know you must think this a sham because of the cruelties of the slave trade, but the servants of the Church have many times protested to the Crown and the Pope. No good can come from so much butchery, for this is not the way in which commerce can flourish and the preaching of the Gospel progress."

"Slavery is not new to us, my friend," Nzinga pointed out, "but there is little meanness in African slavery, and families are never broken apart. There are many good reasons why an African might find himself a slave—an accident which harmed another, a crime committed by a member of his family. Here it is not a disgrace or discredit to be a slave. The master must supply a slave with good food and clothing; he must be given everything needed to celebrate festivals properly; when he is of marriageable age, a spouse must be found. Slaves are part of the family, and the master speaks of them as 'my son' or 'my daughter.' A man cannot be made to cultivate the soil, for that is woman's work, and the black mistress and her female slaves work side by side. Sometimes slaves in their free time are able to accumulate wealth, and freedom can be bought.

"Perhaps our friend Alvares was surprised by my acceptance of slavery. Before the white men came, when we conquered a village, we exterminated it. It is not a light thing to kill a man, even if he is an enemy. Is it not better to sell him and his family to the Europeans, who will pay you and send these enemies to far-off Brazil? Another thing—we have famines here often when the rain gods are angry. Before the white men came, we were forced to let those who could not feed or clothe themselves die. Is it not kinder to give our surplus population a chance to live by selling them to the slave traders? These are things about slavery we can understand."

"But," she continued, "there are some things we cannot understand. The white man's appetite for slaves cannot be satisfied. They ignore the chief's authority, spread falsehoods and start fighting between tribes so that they can get the prisoners of war as slaves. The Portuguese who followed the missionaries are Christian only in the name they disgrace. These things the Mbundu cannot understand.

Sequiera shook his head in disgust. "Many of us believe that slavery of any kind is immoral. In the eyes of God a black soul is as worthy as a white. Slave traders should be refused the Sacraments."

"Ah, but if this accursed war would end," he sighed, "how many marvelous things we could do here in Angola. Land could be cleared to cultivate the coffee which grows wild in the north. In the lowlands great sugar plantations like those in Brazil could be built. And cotton—it grows now even in the streets of Luanda, and your people could be taught to clean it and weave it into fine cloth.

"Does the princess know of the plan to build an overland route to the east coast?" he asked eagerly.

"I believe Governor Corrêa de Souza is a good and sincere man," Nzinga said. "Together we will make these things come to pass."

Later Sequiera repeated the conversation to Alvares. "You are an idealistic fool," the merchant snapped. "Angola will continue as a breeding ground for slaves for Brazil. There will be no plantations and schools and roads built here. To clear the land for plantations would take too many years. Why should any businessman invest his capital and wait for years for coffee trees to begin to bear when in a short time a few glass beads can be turned into a million cruzados in the slave trade? The King cannot see Africa; he is blinded by the glitter of gold and silver from the mines of Mexico and Peru. His treasury grows fat from taxes on the sugar plantations in Brazil and the Caribbean islands. To Portugal, Angola is important only because we ship the slave labor to keep the New World producing wealth."

Alvares' gloomy prediction was forgotten in the excitement that preceded Nzinga's baptism. There was not a European in Luanda who did not squeeze into the great cathedral. The chancel was banked with white blossoms. The bishop intoned the ancient ritual and then bestowed on Nzinga the new name she had chosen in honor of the governor—Ana de Souza. Immediately after the ceremony Dona Ana set out at the head of a gay convoy to rejoin her brother.

Once she was back at the camp on Ndangi Island, surrounded by the sepultures (Mbila) of the royal family of Ndongo, it was difficult to communicate to Ngola-Mbandi all the ideas and impressions she had brought back from Luanda. At least she was able to persuade her brother to ask for a Portuguese priest. Thinking that a black would be more welcome and be better able to work under the difficult conditions of the interior, church officials sent an African, one of the first natives painstakingly educated and ordained in Luanda.

The reactions of Dona Ana and her brother were quite contrary to expectations. They were very upset that a Negro had been sent to propagate the Faith! Did not the Europeans use blacks as slaves? Did their holy book not maintain that the dark-skinned descendants of Ham are forever condemned to be the hewers of wood and the drawers of water, "the servant of servants"? Therefore, it was a logical conclusion to draw that the Portuguese had intended a gross insult to the Mbundu by sending a black priest.

Once the seed of suspicion was planted, it began to grow. The Portuguese prisoners had been released, but the troops around Mbaka, according to reports of spies, were strengthening the fortifications rather than withdrawing. Ngola-Mbandi ventured off the island with a detachment of warriors to scout the situation. After a brief absence, he returned shaken. A number of his subchiefs were working with the Portuguese, and he had barely escaped with his life. An indignant message was sent to Luanda, but the courier came back with the shocking news that Governor João Corrêa de Souza, after a dispute with the Jesuits, had been recalled to Lisbon.

Dona Ana decided to make the difficult journey to Luanda herself. The new governor was fresh from Portugal and did not know about the agreement signed two years before. She would explain the details and insist on his implementing them. But this time there was no viceregal ceremony marking her arrival. She was treated with studied discourtesy.

Alvares was away on business in the Benguela territory, and only her old friend Sequiera sought to comfort her. "We must never give up hope for the future," he said. "Ah, my dear Dona Ana . . ."

She interrupted him, her voice cutting like a blade of Damascus steel. "From this day on I am *Nzinga* again."

After a long pause she told him, "Ngola-Mbandi is not a true son of his father. He will cower on his island like a frightened rat and wait for the Portuguese hawk to swoop down. But suppose that the King of Ndongo looks small, like a scurrying rat, only because the Portuguese hawk is circling so high in the sky. Suppose that when the hawk descends with his talons bared, he finds he had deceived himself and the rat is in fact a rampant lion?" Not all of Sequiera's questions could persuade her to explain what she meant.

Farewells were said shortly thereafter, but they were an empty formality. Sequiera felt that Nzinga had already withdrawn her friendship from all Portuguese. The sensational news that trickled back to Luanda some months later bore out his intuition. Nzinga had welded several dissident Jaga chieftains into a new alliance and with their aid had deposed her brother. Within a few days Ngola-Mbandi was dead of poisoning. Before his end, he entrusted his son to a faithful servant. "Nzinga must never be allowed to approach my son," he warned.

Wild celebrations announced Nzinga's coronation on Ndangi Island, but most spectacular were the bloody rites of her Jaga followers.

Nzinga sat on a ceremonial stool, with a witch doctor on each side whisking her with zebra tails which were stuffed with a potent medicine to ward off death. Her hair was piled high and decorated with knots of *bamba* (whelk or trumpet shells), but otherwise she was dressed as a man.

The medicine men (Ngagas) rubbed her with human fat and anointed her head with a scent made from glands of the civet cat. Then they painted red and white designs on her forehead and belly. Thirty men approached, bearing the king's bows and arrows and peacock feather battle standards, which they laid at her feet. One of their number produced a skull, from which she drank while they clapped their hands and sang songs of praise. They were accompanied by the insistent beating of drums, the bleating of ivory trumpets and the hideous noise of the *puita*, a hollow wooden cylinder covered with sheepskin through which a stick is drawn back and forth.

In the ominous hush that followed, the medicine men threw white powders into an earthen pot sitting on a blazing fire. Then they began to chant, bidding Nzinga to be strong. A *kissengula*, a weapon like a hatchet, was put into her hand, and she was implored to strike down the enemies of her people.

Four men, chosen by the medicine men as sacrificial victims, were brought before her. Two of them she ordered killed in front of the image of Tembo, and two outside the camp. Five cows were beheaded at the foot of the statue, and five beyond the settlement. A long procession of goats, dogs and hens met the same fate. After many hours the blood of the sacrifices was sprinkled into the fire, slowly, so that the flames leaped and grew orange. At last all the carcasses were cooked and eaten with much merriment and carousing.

During the frenzied feasting Nzinga sought out the house of her brother's son. "Would you deny my nephew and me the joy of sharing this happy moment when I ascend the throne of our people?" she asked the devoted and wary servant. With misgivings he brought out the lad, who eagerly entered the murderous embrace of his aunt. As she let his body slump to the ground, she said bitterly, "Thus I have avenged my own son, who today would have been King of Ndongo."

During the next year Nzinga forged a tough alliance of Mbundu and Jaga chieftains. Under her inspirational leadership and brilliant military command they closed all the Portuguese trade routes and confined the whites to their fortified positions on the coast and along the Kwanza and Lukala Rivers. For the Portuguese the situation was insupportable, and with the arrival of reinforcements from Lisbon a grim drive began to break Nzinga's power.

First João de Araujo e Azevedo, commander of the Portuguese invading force, made a last appeal: the lost territories of Ndongo would be restored and the puppet Ngola-Ari, now called Don Felipe, would be abandoned if she acknowledged herself vassal to the King of Portugal and paid an annual tribute like other "good" chieftains.

"I am Ngola of Ndongo," she told the messenger haughtily. "I pay tribute to no one. The Portuguese may come here as traders and missionaries, but not as rulers. As for Ngola-Ari, he may be guardian of the holy places at Mpungu-a-Ndongo, but no chieftain will follow him because he is accursed by the spirits of Kasa, Kasanji, Kinda, Kalandu and all the Ngolas from the beginning of time. Go back and tell your captain that the auguries are in our favor. Black shall be victorious!"

Nzinga knew the Portuguese were greatly outnumbered, but they had the advantage of guns and cannons against bows and arrows. She tried to substitute cleverness for firepower—by attacking with a small force, lulling the Portuguese into overconfidence and then engulfing them with her reserves and by falling on them at dawn when surprise and the early morning dampness would delay ignition of their gunpowder. For the same reason she would stalk a Portuguese column for days, attacking only when it rained. She avoided pitched battles and withdrew quickly if victory was not immediate. In this way she preserved her armies intact, but slowly, inexorably, the invaders pushed the Africans back.

Back from Songo and Muchima, back from Massangano and Dondo and Kambembe, where the River Kwanza tumbles 300 feet in a rainbowed fall, back from Kitambo and Ngoleme on the Lukala River. Whole villages picked up their belongings and moved eastward and northward before the Portuguese advance. The Jaga chieftains Nzenza-a-Ngombe, Bangu-Bangu and Kafuche were caught and beheaded. The Portuguese pursued Nzinga's forces to the gorges of the Ngagela, into which they descended by ropes. The main African force escaped, but Nzinga's sisters, Kambe and Funji, were taken prisoner. Portuguese accounts tell of the girls' arrival in Luanda in 1625 and record their spending many years as guests in the Governor's palace. Both became Christian, adopting the names of Barbara and Engraçia at baptism.

Although the Portuguese had driven Nzinga from Ndongo, they had not heard the last of this remarkable woman. With her powerful army intact, she left the grasslands and moved north into the forests. During the long trek many of Nzinga's people died from starvation and disease. Newborn infants were buried alive so as not to slow down the march. Nzinga was everywhere, exhorting her followers and stiffening their determination.

In 1627 they arrived at the capital of Matamba and without opposition took over that ancient kingdom. Nzinga found the dowager queen, Muongo Matamba, incapable of comprehending the threat of the Portuguese and callously sold her into slavery. Her young daughter was appointed a lady-in-waiting and served faithfully in the court of Nzinga for many years.

As Queen of Matamba, Nzinga had a firm base from which to

harass the Portuguese. To the south lay Kasanje, a powerful federation of Jaga tribes. The Portuguese had ruined the commercial value of Ndongo and now had to reach some 300 miles across the depopulated, arid land to trade for slaves and other commodities with Kasanje. However, all business was conducted at specified points, for the Jagas would allow no soldiers, *pombeiros* or missionaries on their territory.

Over the next ten years the Portuguese made overtures of friendship toward Nzinga, but she would give up neither her sovereign claim to Ndongo nor the Jaga cannibal rites which so disgusted the Europeans. Many times the Portuguese received reports of her death, but they proved to be false rumors, often started by Nzinga herself. All information about her life and movements were kept secret so that she could surprise her enemies. The Portuguese tried to bribe her servants, but they could never break down the fanatic loyalty of Nzinga's followers.

In the late 1630s Governor Francisco de Vasconcellos da Cunha decided to try another tack. He sent back her sisters, accompanied by yet another team of ambassadors—Don Gaspar Borgia, a nobleman fluent in the Mbundu language and customs, and Father Antonio Coelho.

Nzinga was delighted to be reunited with her sisters and eagerly listened to news of Luanda, but when the subject of renewed trade was broached, she was adamant. To the Governor's tempting offers she answered, "You Portuguese may speak with the voices of angels, but your actions are those of devils." She said bitterly, "we have a saying, 'Beware of a man who coos like a ringdove and strikes like a snake.' You think *our* ways are so revolting? It is told that in the year I was born, Paulo Dias de Novais, a great Portuguese hero, met the chiefs of Ndongo in battle near the mountains of Kambembe. When the fighting was over, he cut off the noses of the fallen blacks and sent them to Luanda to prove his victory. Dias was a good Christian, was he not?

"When I was a young girl, my father told me how the Governor, João Furtado de Mendonça, ordered captured chieftains blown from cannons to frighten our warriors. This governor was a man much honored by your king and your priests," she observed sarcastically.

"Let me tell you of something that happened not long ago," she continued. "After a raid in the west one of my warriors was caught devouring a native priest. I have always protected priests, and his actions were strictly against my orders that no priests—white or black—were to be eaten. I had the offender poisoned in secret, and he died before the sun rose—a little trickery, perhaps, but it helped my people to see more clearly that I was wise to forbid the eating of priests. When my orders were disobeyed, the culprit died. So, you see, I continue my work for the Church. In my heart I still hold dear the teachings of Jesus, but my people would never accept a Christian queen. To lead them I must embrace their religion."

The two ambassadors were fascinated, but they returned from Matamba empty-handed. When he heard their report, the Governor threw up his hands. "That woman was born for the ruin of Angola," he muttered.

During the next few years, that was just the way it seemed. Nzinga's friendship became particularly important to the Portuguese because of growing threats from the Dutch, whose secret agents planted harmful rumors everywhere among the native rulers. The rivalry between the Dutch and the Portuguese in Angola and the Kongo was but one scene in a world-wide struggle for colonial power. They clashed in Brazil, on the west coast of Africa and in the Orient. Encouraged by Portugal's weakness, Dutch ships had become increasingly aggressive, and the Angolan coastal towns of Luanda and Benguela nervously anticipated an invasion. Aside from their hunger for power over faraway lands, the Portuguese had another reason for hating the Dutch—the Portuguese were Roman Catholics, and the Dutch had rejected "the true faith" for "the Protestant heresy." Dutch "missionaries of the Devil" were spreading their "false doctrines of Protestantism" and distributing inflammatory tracts and heretical religious materials among the blacks whom the Portuguese had converted to Catholicism. The

Africans were well disposed to listen because Dutch traders offered better commercial bargains and higher-quality goods from northern Europe.

In 1641, the Duke of Braganza became King João IV, and Portuguese all over the world hoped that their new leader would throw off Spanish influence, end the wars with Holland and reaffirm Portugal as one of the world's leading powers. When word of João's coronation reached Luanda, the inhabitants staged a wild celebration in honor of their new king. Suddenly, in the midst of their rejoicing, a large Dutch fleet appeared in the harbor. The panic-stricken residents began to flee, and Governor Pedro Cezar de Menezes tried to rally his 900 white troops for a stand against the invaders.

As he issued frantic orders, Bishop de Soveral broke into military headquarters. "The Hollanders have beached their ships between the two forts and out of range of either of their cannons. I have learned that they have 2,000 troops and 900 sailors who can be called in as reserves. This is no quick raid. They have come to stay. You will bring disaster on us all if you resist."

"Pull out without a fight?" the Governor sputtered. "The honor of Portugal . . . I vow by São Paulo, patron of Luanda . . ."

The Bishop cut him off impatiently. "With your few hundred men and guns of small caliber, you will be decimated by the Dutch and then exterminated by the vengeful chieftains. Defeat will end Portugal's chances in Angola forever. If we retire with our strength intact, we can still hold the interior territories until relief arrives from Lisbon."

Offering only token resistance, Cezar de Menezes withdrew some fifteen miles to the northeast to the Bengo River Valley, where rich Portuguese farms offered a base for future operations. At a cost of three men, the Dutch took Luanda—thirty ships, almost a hundred cannons and much booty. Expecting to find a squalid settlement of slave markets and thatched mud huts, the conquerors were astonished at the riches, comfort and cultural achievements of Luanda.

While his soldiers looted "Papist churches" and burned their "heathenish saints and idols," Dutch Commander Jeems Hindersson lost no time in sending a flying squadron to make contact with Nzinga. He had guessed correctly that she would take advantage of the situation to move out of Matamba and reclaim Ndongo. Their forces met near the Dande River, and the Queen warmly embraced the chief Dutch emissary, Gaspar Croasen. "The enemy of my enemy is my friend," she said.

The negotiations which followed were not difficult, for both sides had much to gain from cooperation. The Dutch recognized Nzinga's right to Ndongo and invited the Mbundu people to reclaim their land. It was far better to deal with a contented, flourishing native population, they reasoned, than with the sullen remnants who had remained under the Portuguese. Black warriors reoccupying their lost territory would keep the Portuguese in the interior very busy. Both as a practical measure and as a guard of honor, a large Dutch force was put at the disposal of Queen Nzinga.

Amid wild rejoicing, Nzinga and her followers reoccupied Mbaka and pursued the retreating Portuguese. Her assignment was to keep them bottled up in the old fort at Massangano.

As he moved south with Nzinga, the Dutch liaison officer and Captain Füller, the military attaché, sent a series of dispatches which were of more than routine military interest. After her withdrawal to Matamba, Nzinga's life had been shrouded in secrecy, and so these accounts gave white men additional insights into life among the Mbundu and their Jaga allies.

"When the Queen Nzinga comes on a scene, everyone falls on his knees, kisses the ground and claps his hands. If women are present, they express their delight by beating their open mouths with the palms of their hands as they utter short cries of 'ah! ah! ah!'"

"Nzinga is advised by a group of subchiefs, or Sobas, and a council of elders. However, she is an excellent strategist, a fearless warrior and a wise and cunning politician."

"When we stop for a few days, the blacks cut down trees and build a great circle of twelve gates. Each captain is responsible for the defense of an assigned gate. In the center of the compound, Nzinga's hut is erected and surrounded by a triple hedge of thorns. Shelters are built close together, and bows, arrows, darts and spears stand ready outside the entrances. All through the night the watchmen keep the drums throbbing and pound the *tavale* until their fingers must wear down to stumps. Even more remarkable, only our poor Netherlanders seem to awake with headaches from the incessant noise!"

"Have you not often wondered how these blacks communicate with each other during a far-flung battle action, coordinating their movements and sending intelligence from one contingent to another? Before yesterday's battle I observed Queen Nzinga and her commanders lay their plans. Each captain and subchief has a distinctive sound on a particular musical instrument like a drum or rattle or trumpet made from animal horn. Captains are able to communicate by a complex code of sound."

"Since local custom does not allow a woman to rule as chief, Nzinga dresses always in male clothing and is addressed as 'King.' In her entourage are kept 50 or 60 stalwart young men dressed as females who constitute her 'harem.' Her morals are not doubtful; they are nonexistent."

"On the morning of an attack, Nzinga mounts a high scaffold. She is past 60, but lithe as the most agile youngster in her camp. She is dressed in men's clothing with animal skins hanging in front and behind. At her feet are placed a knife, a double bell called Ngonge, which is the symbol of war, and a silver chest bearing the bones of her ancestors. Then she proceeds to harangue her warriors, reminding them of the injustices inflicted by the Portuguese, invoking the sacred symbols, pulling them to her purpose with her magnetic voice. Some of the best and bravest of her warriors, splendidly attired and fully armed, offer themselves for sacrifice. Nzinga sticks a feather through her nose as a symbol of war and hacks off the head of the first victim. After she drinks of his blood, her captains do the same. Meanwhile, the assemblage sets up a deafening clatter and clang by beating together eating utensils, weapons—anything that will make a noise. In this way Nzinga inspires her men to great feats of heroism. Indeed, cowardice is a bad policy, for faint-hearted soldiers who turn their backs in battle are killed and eaten."

"Nzinga insists a king cannot be bound by ties of blood. She is cruel and crafty. And yet she is so generously valiant that she never hurt a Portuguese after quarter was given and commanded all her soldiers and slaves the like. I saw her genuinely saddened by the news of a recent incident on the Kwanza River. The sick and aged from the Bengo farms had been loaded on to pinnaces and were being rowed upstream to Massangano. With them were launches filled with documents, records, deeds and books from Luanda. Our Dutch and black allies fell on the refugees, murdering every one, and then dumped the bodies and the books and papers into the river for the nurture and edification of the crocodiles. There were tears in Nzinga's eyes when she heard the report; yet this is the same woman I have seen eat human flesh with apparent relish!"

In 1643 news came from Europe that an armistice between Holland and Portugal had been signed. Accordingly, Cornelis Nieulandt, Dutch governor of Luanda, sought to secure peace with the Portuguese besieged in Massangano by Nzinga. According to the terms of the agreement finally reached, the Portuguese were allowed to return to their farms in the Bengo River Valley.

Nzinga and her chieftains, flanked by her Dutch bodyguard, watched impassively as the refugees streamed out of Fort Massangano. An eerie silence blanketed the scene as the former conquerors stumbled along the dusty path, many too racked with fever or enfeebled by starvation to walk without assistance.

Once they were established on the Bengo River, confidence came flooding back to the Portuguese. Food was plentiful, Governor Menezes had established a workable system of regulations and the Portuguese troops scattered through the interior had added their strength to the Bengo River colony. Cezar de Menezes trusted Governor Nieulandt and did not set up a system of military protection.

This idyllic arrangement lasted only five months. Nieulandt became ill and was succeeded by Hans Molt. War hawks among his advisers convinced him that Menezes was laying plans to recapture Luanda. Nzinga's role in the decision was uncertain, but Molt knew that she could be counted on to carry out any action against the Portuguese. At dawn 150 well-armed Dutch and their native auxiliaries attacked. Many Portuguese were killed, and 200 men were taken prisoner. The victors were distracted by silver, gold and other rich goods to loot, thus enabling Cezar de Menezes and a large group of Portuguese to flee through the bush back to the safety of Massangano.

Assessing the situation, the Portuguese realized that they had to hold on in the interior until help arrived from the outside. The Dutch did not pursue them, but relied on Nzinga and her allies to keep them in line.

How were the Portuguese to keep alive? In time they worked out a *modus vivendi* with the Dutch, who were willing to trade food and supplies for slaves. Portuguese expeditions were sent eastward to the plateau country to Mbalundu, and south toward Benguela. Nzinga noted ironically that the former masters of the Angolan slave trade were now its servants. Slaves were no longer an adornment of prosperity, but a brutal necessity of survival for the Portuguese. The glorious conquistadores were reduced to *pombeiros*.

Meanwhile, events in Africa began to have their effect in Portuguese Brazil and Spanish America. The sharp reduction in the supply of slaves caused severe economic problems, and before long the sugar plantation and mill owners and the overseers of the mines began to demand action. As a result, several attempts were made to recapture Angola from the Dutch, but they were unsuccessful.

When they received reports of the Portuguese activities, the Dutch realized that they had made a serious error in allowing the Portuguese to maintain a foothold in the hinterland. It was clear that Massangano had to be taken before further aid from Portugal and the rich colony in Brazil could turn the tide. In line with their new "get tough" policy, the Dutch constructed Fort Mols at the mouth of the Kwanza River and another strong point further upstream. In this way access from Massangano to the ocean was barred.

At the same time, Nzinga unleashed an all-out assault. The desperate Portuguese anticipated this move, and in January of 1646, before her chieftains could gather their full strength, Gaspar Borges de Madureira broke out of the Massangano encirclement and attacked Nzinga's Dande River camp. Taken by surprise, the natives left 2,000 dead on the field. Nzinga's sisters were among the many captives herded back to Massangano. Soon afterwards Dona Engraçia was strangled for a suspected act of treachery. Dona Barbara was kept in captivity for eleven more years.

In March a punitive expedition organized by Sottomaior, who had become the new Portuguese governor, dealt Nzinga's forces another blow with the aid of the puppet king of Ndongo, Ngola-Ari. However, the old Amazon was soon back in the field. By September she had inflicted a severe defeat on the troops defending Massangano but, respecting Dutch advice, did not move in to take the fort itself. A few weeks later she led a furious attack on Muchima, but withdrew when she foresaw a trap threatened by a relief regiment from Massangano.

Reinforced by the King of the Kongo and fresh Dutch arms, Nzinga ended Portuguese resistance at Kawala.

It was at this moment of triumph and promise of a bright future that two ominous events took place that were to bar Nzinga's progress toward her lifelong goal—throwing off the yoke of the white invaders and re-establishing Ndongo as a proudly independent kingdom.

The ruling Jaga chief of the neighboring kingdom of Kasanje had become distressed by the bad effect the war was having on his income from the slave trade. Consequently, he went back on his agreement with Nzinga and once more threw his support to the

Portuguese. This act signaled the crumbling of the African alliance led by Nzinga.

And in Lisbon, King João IV decided that the Portuguese must regain Angola at any cost. As a result, a well-outfitted armada left Rio de Janeiro in Portuguese Brazil on May 12, 1648. Salvador Correia de Sá Benevides commanded the expeditionary force, and he was a man whose past record equipped him for the difficult job ahead.

The preparations for the expeditionary force, the journey itself, and de Sá's first landing in Africa at Kikombo Bay were accomplished with so much secrecy that Nzinga and her Dutch allies knew nothing of the Portuguese counteroffensive. Their first warning came when some warrior allies of Nzinga brought into camp three captured Portuguese. It was evident that they were not of the bedraggled Massangano defenders.

Nzinga sent immediately for Symon Pieterszoon, commander of the Dutch garrison in Luanda, who with 225 of his best men had recently joined Nzinga in a sweep down the Kwanza River from Massangano. The Portuguese revealed nothing under questioning, but when Pierterszoon and his lieutenants arrived, the dispatch cases were opened. The captives proved to be couriers put ashore at Kikombo. They carried letters from de Sá urging the Massangano garrison to break out and attack Luanda from the rear while he made a frontal assault on the fortresses guarding the bay.

"The Portuguese at Massangano cannot help your general," Nzinga chortled. "They are too busy counting their dead." Just that day she and Pierterszoon had ambushed and wiped out a force of 125 men caught reconnoitering beyond the fortifications.

Pieterszoon immediately sent a warning message to the men in charge of Luanda, Cornelis Ouman and Adriaen Lens. Unfortunately, by the time it arrived, de Sá had already landed on the beaches.

As they marshaled their warriors and began a forced march to Luanda, Pierterszoon reassured Nzinga. "The fortresses are well supplied with food and water. I myself worked out the master plan.

There are enough guns and ammunition to hold out till the devil takes de Sá. The Portuguese in Massangano don't know that de Sá needs their help, and, for a little while anyhow, they won't know we have pulled out. It's all very simple—Ouman and Lens can stall till we get there, and we'll bring de Sá greetings from Massangano—but not quite what he expects!"

Imagine Pierterszoon's astonishment and disgust when messengers met them with news that the Dutch had surrendered Luanda. He read to Nzinga from the dispatches: "The cannons guarding the Morro have proved unreliable. Many gun carriages blew up and barrels burst when the guns were fired."

Pieterszoon howled in rage. "I myself commanded all ordnance tested regularly, but those pinchpenny, mite-brained directors countermanded my orders! A waste of money, was it?"

He read further in a voice hoarse with anger: "As you know, the troop ships from Europe have not arrived this year. You have absented yourself upcountry with a crack company. Therefore, in our opinion, there were not enough soldiers left to man our extensive fortifications and meet the Portuguese challenge. In part, we must admit, our judgment was warped by a Portuguese trick. De Sá had thousands of troops rowed ashore, and from the Morro we could see hundreds more still lined up on board the ships, their battalion flags flying, bands playing, awaiting their turn on the landing craft. To our chagrin, we later learned that de Sá had used dummies to fool us into overestimating his strength."

Pieterszoon turned from Nzinga and spat in the dust. "They didn't have to be tricked. Those white-livered, yellow-bellied sniveling cowards had no guts to fight!"

"Accordingly, we have accepted de Sá's most generous terms of surrender," the dispatch continued. "If we evacuate Angola, the Portuguese will provide the ships to take us back to Holland or to the Dutch coast of Brazil. We may keep our slaves or sell them before leaving. A most gentlemanly victor, de Sá has personally guaranteed that neither the population nor the garrison will be molested or insulted.

"As for your situation, de Sá has decided that if you accept the terms of surrender, you are directed to join us in Luanda to await transport. If you choose to continue the fight, we are forbidden to assist you in any way. De Sá has graciously allowed five days."

"Do Ouman and Lens think that I, Symon Pieterszoon, will go slinking into Luanda with my tail between my legs!" he roared.

"My friend," Nzinga said, "the enraged elephant stampedes into the trap. Now you must make yourself cunning and wary like the leopard."

For the rest of the day Pieterszoon and the old Queen discussed his situation. She urged him to throw his lot in with the Africans and continue the guerrilla struggle against the Portuguese. However, it became clear that there was no hope for the future in such a course of action. Holland would not reinforce him with men or supplies, and he could look forward only to gradual attrition of his company. Finally, he too would die of disease or wounds far from home. At last, even Nzinga urged Pieterszoon to return with the Dutch from Luanda, although she knew she would miss her rough, valiant comrade-at-arms.

Pieterszoon brought his fist down on the makeshift camp table. "So be it! But we march on to the Portuguese ships with only our swords. We leave with you all our supplies, our muskets and cannons, the ammunition, everything, and may you make a hell here on earth for those Popish idolators!"

Soon after the liberation of Luanda, de Sá called a meeting of the town council to discuss punishment for the chieftains who had not remained loyal. Feelings against Nzinga were especially bitter because she had embraced the Dutch and strengthened the backbone of resistance among all the lesser chiefs.

De Sá generously came to her defense: "With all her faults, this Amazon fights for what she believes to be her tribal lands. Her ancestors once ruled all of Angola. Is she so very different from any politician, ancient or modern, who professes moral and religious principles, but acts according to his own interests? While she was at war with us, she could maintain her power and prestige among the tribes only by enthusiastically supporting their heathen passions. I am sure that when the Queen remembers her days in Luanda and thinks back on the good fathers who taught her catechism, her conscience is revolted by cannibalism, infanticide and bloody sacrifices. She became a Christian of her own free will and therefore assumed certain obligations. We will be doing God's work if we help her and her Mbundu people toward civilization."

Not entirely convinced, one of the magistrates said, "In any event, we have too much to rebuild to divert our money and our efforts in military expeditions. If we send out our garrison to fight Nzinga, we leave ourselves open to new attacks by the Dutch."

After a lively debate the council decided to send Captain Ruy Pegado with rich presents and an offer of friendship. While their ambassador sought to follow Nzinga's will-o'-the-wisp trail into the interior, the Portuguese tackled their many other problems. The King of Kongo and other dissident chieftains had to be brought into line, the slave-gathering system rebuilt and commercial relations with their countrymen in Brazil re-established.

When Captain Pegado finally caught up with Nzinga, he found her as intransigent as ever. She spurned all Portuguese gifts and treaties. One of the dispatches that reached the Luanda council said: "The chief reason why the savage tribes and Negroes of this kingdom got on very well with the Dutch and why they therefore would like to see them back again is this: the Dutch have always let them peacefully possess their lands without ever trying to interfere with their crops, or allowing any white man to disturb them in their dwellings or elsewhere, as the Portuguese have done and still do daily, robbing and molesting those people as if they were not under His Majesty's protection."

Another message from Pegado reminded the Bishop that Capuchin monks of the Order of St. Francis had been active all through the Kongo and Matamba during the years of the Dutch occupation. Fellow Catholics but rivals of the Jesuits, the Capuchin fathers had ignored the order of the King of Portugal banning them from the Kongo and Matamba. The Dutch, although Protestant, had been more lenient about their activities.

Captain Pegado wrote: "These long-bearded Italians have been active in Matamba. They have made many new converts and have successfully brought back into the fold lapsed Christians and natives poisoned by the false doctrines of the Dutch. Queen Nzinga has expressed a strong desire to be reunited with the Capuchin Father Antonio Laudati de Gaeta. The Council may find Nzinga more willing to accept our overtures if Father Antonio is allowed to rejoin her."

Shortly after the frustrated Pegado left, a group of captured Portuguese were brought to Nzinga. She ordered her men to cut the tough vines with which they were bound. Suddenly, she uttered a sharp cry of recognition. "Sequiera, my dear friend, my heart is flooded with sunshine!" It was indeed her acquaintance from Luanda, now a chief inspector of missions in the interior of Angola.

She waved the other prisoners back to their guarded camp, but ordered food for her friend. Mutombo cakes made from ground mandioc flour appeared, along with ground-nut and pumpkin stew and palm wine. Nzinga pressed fruits into his hand until he laughingly protested he could eat nothing more. Then they passed back and forth a cola nut, bitter at first gulp, but required by etiquette at social meetings.

Nzinga drank in the news of Luanda. She was particularly concerned about her sister Barbara and begged Sequiera to try to arrange for her release. Then the Queen personally conducted him on a tour of her capital. When she left him at the prisoners' compound, she summoned the captain of the guard. "With the first light set your men to build a house," she ordered. "Thatch the roof carefully and when you are done, paint the inside white."

The next evening Nzinga took Sequiera to the gleaming new hut. "This is a chapel for you, my friend. You are a lay Jesuit priest, and you must say mass for the others. So, you see, I still respect the God of the Christians."

That night Sequiera discovered two of his fellow prisoners plotting an escape. He failed to dissuade them, and he feared that the unpredictable Queen would massacre the remaining prisoners whether or not they were successful. He informed Nzinga, and she agreed to spare their lives.

However, she could not resist turning the incident to her advantage. She called together her subjects and with her medicine men went into a short seance. Soon she emerged from the spell of the Ngagas' hypnotic incantations and magic powders. She screeched to the mob that the tribal ancestors had revealed to her that two of the Portuguese were attempting to escape. The guards were informed, and caught the prisoners trying to cut through the palm cane paling behind the jail. Nzinga's credit with her people soared to new heights.

Some time after Sequiera and the others were released, Nzinga's best general, Mani Dongo, attacked a small tribe on the Kongo border. The warriors leveled the village and brought back some tokens for their Queen. Among them was a beautifully wrought crucifix. The sight of the cross brought tears to old Nzinga's eyes, and with her own hands she fashioned a small shrine in which she installed the crucifix.

That night she consulted her ancestors for guidance. The medicine men prepared potions and chanted the age-old prayers while she communed privately with the spirits. Later she emerged from her hut, visibly shaken, and announced, "My brother, my father, Kasa and Kasanji, Kinda and Kalandu and all the ancestors of our ancestors have told me they suffer eternal torments. Karia-pemba, the evil devil, has promised to release them if their sister returns to the faith of the white men in which she was baptized. Only then will God the Most High, Nzambi-Mpungu, look on them with smiles and relieve their agonies."

None would dare oppose her will, and for many days and nights the *kraals* resounded with joyful music and dancing. Soon afterward, the Capuchin friar Antonio de Gaeta arrived with Captain

Manuel Freis Peixoto to conduct negotiations for a peace treaty. The boundaries between the Portuguese territories and Nzinga's kingdom were clearly defined—the Lukala River on the west, the Kwango on the east and the Kwanza on the south. To the north lay the Kongo, with which Nzinga had friendly relations. It was decided that a resident captain would remain with Nzinga in her Matamba capital to promote Portuguese trading interests and settle commercial disputes. In addition, Nzinga offered a ransom for the return of her sister Barbara.

The Portuguese Governor of Angola, Luis de Souza Chichorro, wrote back to his new friend, "the esteemed Dona Ana de Souza," expressing his great joy at her having "abjured the apostasy in which she seemed for a time rooted and ceased her abominable cruelties."

In exchange for 130 slaves, Dona Barbara returned to Matamba with an escort of three Portuguese officers. Nzinga sent back a message to the Governor regretting "her ingratitude despite many kindnesses received." As to the still unresolved question of paying annual tribute to the Portuguese, the wily Nzinga pointed out: "No ancestor of mine had done so. It would be indecent to ask me, a Christian ruler, to be more submissive than heathen kings."

To supply the ever-growing demand for slaves, the Portuguese needed Nzinga's cooperation. In the past they had never been able to force her into vassalage. With this in mind, they dropped their demands for tribute.

No sooner was a final agreement reached than the new puppet king of Ndongo, son of Ngola-Ari, denounced the Portuguese. Now that Nzinga and the whites were on friendly and equal terms, his dream of establishing himself at the head of a restored Kingdom of Ndongo had become impossible. Portuguese landowners captured his subjects for work on estates, and traders commandeered his men as carriers to bear goods to the slave markets in Kasanje. Was this his reward for loyalty in the Dutch wars? A direct appeal to the King of Portugal resulted in a royal order to free all enslaved Ndongo subjects and to pay the carriers for their labor. However, the Portuguese in Angola, long experienced in ignoring or bypassing royal orders, did not mend their ways.

Nzinga had little time to gloat over the troubles of the son of her old enemy Ngola-Ari. She spent most of her time supervising the construction of the Church of Santa Maria de Matamba. There in 1657, when she was seventy-five years old, Father Antonio rebaptized her. Then she disbanded her "harem" and married one of her "wives," a slave youth named Don Salvatore, in a solemn church ceremony. He was called "husband to the King," for Nzinga would not give up her title.

Her sister Barbara was also married in Catholic rites—to Don Antonio Carrasco Nzinga a Mona, a foster brother of the Queen and general of her armies.

Under the continued influence of the Capuchin monks, Nzinga abolished human sacrifice in her kingdom. Several new chapels were built, one within the royal palace enclosure dedicated to her patron, Santa Ana. She also ordered strict enforcement of the provisions of the Portuguese treaty. On the first occasion that one of her chieftains violated the terms of peace, she had his head cut off and sent to Luanda as proof of her steadfastness.

During her last three years of life, Dona Ana spent much of her time devoutly attending church services with her large court of maidens. She sent an embassy to Rome to petition the Pope for additional missionaries. When the Pontiff's answer arrived, it was publicly read in church. At a festival in honor of the occasion, Dona Ana and the ladies of her train performed a mock battle in the dress and armor of Amazons. Almost eighty, Dona Ana showed as much strength and agility as a twenty-five-year-old, one observer reported.

In 1663, Father Cavazzi was called hurriedly to administer last rites to the eighty-one-year-old "King." By her order her body was shown to her sorrowing subjects clothed in a Capuchin habit, complete with crucifix and rosary. She was buried in the Church of Santa Ana arrayed in royal robes ornamented with precious stones, her bow and arrow in her hand.

Throughout the years many chieftains have followed Nzinga's example of fighting for the right to govern themselves, but today Portugal still controls Angola. Slaves are no longer shipped to Brazil, but many visitors have come back with stories of the forced labor required of the native population. With this labor, white settlers have built the coffee plantations and established the thriving exports of cotton and sugar that early idealists like Sequiera predicted. However, few of the benefits of this modern agriculture have trickled through to the black Angolans. Recent discoveries of oil, as well as potentially rich mineral deposits, have only hardened Portugal's determination to hold on in Angola. To strengthen this grip, some 40,000 Portuguese soldiers must keep constantly on the alert.

Unlike their ancient queen, rebellious Angolans no longer fight with spears, bows and arrows. They are supplied with modern weapons by other African countries who are eager to eject the last of the great colonial powers. Recent uprisings have been ruthlessly extinguished, but the flame of freedom then springs up in another part of the country. The United Nations has passed resolutions condemning Portuguese colonial policies in Africa, and the newly independent countries of that continent have pledged their aid to Angolan guerrillas.

Those freedom fighters, many living in hiding in jungle clearings just across the Congo border, hold fast to the example of Nzinga. Her courage in the face of the superiority of Portuguese weapons, her cunning as an adversary and her unwavering determination through long, dark years of exile all serve as inspiration for today's Angolans who fight to break the grip of their Portuguese colonial masters. Perhaps with the aid of other African countries these descendants of Nzinga will at last fulfill the old queen's dream of a strong and free Angola, dealing with other countries as an equal, proud of its past and ambitious for its future.

SAMUEL AJAYI CROWTHER

ALTHOUGH it was early in the morning, the Yoruba village of Oshogun was bustling with activity under the bright sun. In the marketplace the women were busy preparing breakfast, the little children tumbling and playing round their feet. As the men collected their farming tools or adjusted their looms for the day's weaving, they grumbled that the meal was not yet ready. In the yard of his home, thirteen-year-old Ajayi clucked at his chickens, smiling as they gobbled the feed he was scattering.

Suddenly, without warning, the air filled with shrieks. Looking up in terror, Ajayi stared into dark, menacing faces surrounding him on every side. Were these the dreaded Fulani slave raiders? He stumbled over the squawking chickens as he turned to flee and then, half choking, was caught up short by the lasso which one of the raiders had skillfully whipped around his neck.

Ajayi stared wildly about him as he was dragged toward the marketplace to be roped to the other villagers already captured. There were his mother and two sisters, frantically calling his name as he tripped among the wounded and dead, whose bodies seemed everywhere. His cousin clutched at him wordlessly as Ajayi was pulled along. Then, in horror, he saw one of the Fulanis tearing an infant from its mother's arms, dashing the baby to the ground as he bound the screaming woman to her fellow captives. Curls of smoke from houses already put to the torch drifted upward in the bright air. Ajayi struggled to free himself of the thongs cutting into his arms and ankles, but his frenzied thrashing about brought no escape, only unbearable pain as the blood oozed from his raw skin.

On that tragic day in 1821, the destruction of Oshogun marked the fall of yet another peaceful Yoruba village to the slave-raiding Mohammedan Fulanis of the north. Here in Yorubaland, lying between the west branch of the Niger River and the seacoast, the slave trade, probably more than anywhere else in Africa, took a constant toll. The area was deeply torn by civil wars among the tribes. Slave raids, both from the northern Fulanis and among the various tribes of Yorubaland, were common. Some of the captured slaves were kept for use in Africa by the various raiding tribes; others were sold and shipped to the Americas, where the demand was seemingly inexhaustible; still others were sent north across the desert to Arab lands. Whole villages, like Ajayi's Oshogun, disappeared under the blow of a successful slave raid.

The long slave march to Isehin began early in the afternoon of the raid. Ajayi's eyes blurred with tears as he limped past the burning hut where his father's loom stood smoldering. "Where is my father now?" he thought sorrowfully. "Has he been captured or even killed?" His heart was heavy as he glimpsed the half-finished gaily colored fabrics his father had been weaving for the king of Ilorin. As Ajayi recognized the bodies of some of Oshogun's 3,000 fighting men, he knew he would never see his father again. Nor was he likely to see other relatives or childhood friends. The captives had been parceled out among the victors, and in many cases, as Ajayi wrote later, "a family was divided between three or four enemies, who each led him away to see each other no more."

The file of slaves straggled through a break in the fence whose four-mile length enclosing Oshogun had proved so ineffective as protection. One of the Fulani guards laughed out loud as he thrust his bulk against the broken timbers. At that moment a Yoruba prisoner, having stealthily worked his way loose from his bonds, flew like an arrow from the slave line toward a nearby clump of trees. As two Fulanis leaped after the fugitive and seized him, a long moan of anguish burst from the throats of the slaves. In no time the captors had cut down a young tree with two large forked branches and, pushing the Yoruba slave back into the line behind Ajayi, fastened the forked limbs to the captive's neck. The only way he could walk now was to bear the heavy trunk in his arms ahead of him. It was not long before he began to stumble under the weight. Young Ajayi turned to whisper to his fellow prisoner. "Pick up the tree trunk. Let it rest on my shoulder." And so the weary march proceeded.

The months of slavery which followed blended into one long, continuous nightmare. Bartered at different times for tobacco, rum and a horse, Ajayi could scarcely distinguish one day from another. Once, in twenty-four hours, he became the property of three different masters. At one point he was bought by a Mohammedan woman and marched to the Gulf of Guinea coast. His body, ravaged by dysentery, and his sick soul could stand no more. That night he tried to strangle himself but found that he could not pull the noose tight enough. His mistress, annoyed by his mournful face and poor health, heaved a sigh of relief when she was able to find a new buyer. As he was traded from one owner to the next, Ajayi was finally marched off to Lagos, one hand chained to his neck. There he was sold to the Portuguese and, chained with 186 other slaves, was put aboard a sailing vessel, the *Esperanza Felix* (the "Happy Hope").

In the dank hold, pressed tightly by other bodies, Ajayi craned his head to look at his fellow captives. "Where are we going? What will become of us?" he cried.

A voice answered him in Yoruba. "Far over the waters, my son. To the fields where white masters will put us to labor." Ajayi peered at the middle-aged man who had replied. "Who are you?" he asked. "How do you know?"

"I am Lagunju of the village of Igbom. I was a slave for the white man in Lagos, but I escaped. Then I was recaptured by raiders while seeking my way back to my wife and children. I know the white demons and what they do to our people. We will sail over the great waters. Many of us will die of disease or thirst on the voyage. But perhaps that is better than what will happen to those who survive, for I have heard they will break their bodies and their hearts toiling in the green fields of sugarcane in far-off islands."

Ajayi shuddered. Was this the "extraordinary destiny" that awaited him? When he was born, his father and mother had taken him to the priests so that Ifa, the god of prophecy, could advise them about his future. There they had learned that this was an extraordinary baby, who could not be dedicated to any idol. Speaking in Ifa's voice, the medicine men had foretold that Ajayi was to become an *alùja*, an outstanding and famous person who could be consecrated only to the service of Olorun, the Creator. In his present misery, Ajayi smiled bitterly as he thought of the prophecy.

Visions of his happy childhood drifted before Ajayi's eyes. When he was eight, he had received a piece of land near his father's farm, seven miles out of the village. There Ajayi had learned to cultivate yams, and there he had become the *baba*, or leader, of forty of his age-mates. The boys had formed a happy band, sharing their work and play, teasing one another, growing toward young manhood together. Ajayi's heart contracted as he remembered the time Abidu and Olunlade, his closest friends, had solemnly honored him for his bravery. The house of Ajayi's father had caught fire, and the entire family, in the turmoil and excitement, had left the revered ancestor figures in the flames. But Ajayi had rushed over the porch into the house and carried the sacred figures to safety.

Lagunju's voice broke into Ajayi's revery. "Listen! Something is happening above!" The slaves huddled closer together as the sound of scuffling footsteps, the sharp reports of shots and shouting voices came from the deck overhead. What new enemy was this? In a short while, strange white men swarmed into the hold, and the slaves, unable to understand what was happening, were pushed up to the deck and transferred to another ship which now lay alongside the *Esperanza Felix*.

Obscured by clouds, the moon shone dimly over the slaves as they stumbled on the deck of the new vessel. Ajayi clutched at Lagunju and pointed to chunks of meat hanging from hooks in the pale light. "The flesh of our brothers!" he gasped. "It is true, then, that the white demons kill black men to eat their flesh and to use their blood for red dye!"

"And there, in the corner, see how the heads are piled up!" replied Lagunju, his voice trembling. Neither of the two Yorubas realized that what they saw were sides of pork for the ship's provisions, and that the severed black heads were in reality a pyramid of cannonballs.

The next morning the ship's captain ordered all hands to assemble on deck. Speaking to the wondering slaves through interpreters, he said: "I am Captain Henry Leeke of the British Navy. You are aboard Her Majesty's warship *Myrmidon* on patrol in the Gulf of

Guinea to intercept slave ships, and it is the good fortune of all of us that the *Esperanza Felix* fell into our hands last night. You are no longer slaves, but we cannot yet return you to shore. It is our duty to continue our patrol to seek out other slavers and liberate their captives. After a time, you will be landed in freedom."

As the captain spoke, the Portuguese slave-owner of the *Esperanza Felix* was brought on board in chains. Ajayi fixed his eyes on his former captor, and his heart exploded with all the cruelties and indignities of the last few months. With a scream of rage, the boy leaped forward and began to flail the man's head with his fists. The other slaves roared their approval, but the British sailors, laughing, pulled the youth away from his victim and hurried the Portuguese below deck.

Ajayi's outburst had caught the attention of some of the sailors, who were delighted by the young slave's show of spirit. During the two and a half months that the *Myrmidon* patrolled the coast, Ajayi served the sailors as their cabin boy. His bright, intelligent ways and quick grasp of his duties made him a favorite. The sailors encouraged Ajayi's halting attempts to speak English, and the lad soon became the unofficial interpreter for the Yorubas on board the vessel.

The hot June sun beat down on the *Myrmidon* one afternoon when Ajayi was resting quietly on deck. A sailor smiled at the drowsy boy and said, "Ajayi, you will soon be leaving us. No more loafing around, my lad—I've heard that we'll be landing at Freetown in Sierra Leone in another week."

"Freetown? Where is that? Is it near Oshogun, my home?"

"No, my boy. It is hundreds of miles from where we found you at Lagos. That's where all our freed slaves go. You'll start your new life in Sierra Leone." He told Ajayi that Sierra Leone had been established by an Englishman, Granville Sharp, as a home for freed slaves as far back as 1767.

Ajayi was still puzzled. "Why are you not taking us back to our own land?" he asked.

"Because," the sailor answered, "if you and the other slaves were set free at Lagos, you would undoubtedly be recaptured immediately by slave traders, since we British have no control on that part of the coast." Perhaps he was embarrassed to add that there was an admiralty court at Sierra Leone where the British Navy received prize money for every freed slave. Thus British patrol ships returned all their liberated captives to Sierra Leone, no matter from where they had originally come. The population of Sierra Leone had therefore come to include the native inhabitants and blacks from many other parts of western Africa, including numerous Yorubas like Ajayi.

"I understand," said Ajayi. He hesitated before his next question, and then decided to take the plunge. "But I still do not know why you are helping us. You are white and so are the Portuguese. Are your tribes at war?"

The sailor laughed. "In a way," he replied. "My country, England, stopped buying and selling slaves long ago, in 1807. God teaches us that slavery is wrong, but many other men, both black and white, have not yet learned God's truth. We are trying to teach them. We must show them that there is as much profit in palm oil, timber, beeswax and ivory as in human bodies."

"Will I learn about your God?" Ajayi asked.

"Yes, you will. The people who will teach you about our God are called missionaries. I am sure you will go to a mission school, perhaps to my friends Mr. and Mrs. Davey in Bathurst. If you meet them, give them a greeting from me."

It was indeed Ajayi's good fortune to be sent to Bathurst soon after landing at Freetown. A whole new life opened before his eager eyes. Everything was fresh and exciting; both his childhood days at Oshogun and his tortured months of slavery receded into forgetfulness. His missionary teachers were astonished at the energy with which Ajayi threw himself into each new experience and at the speed with which he learned. One of the schoolmasters taught him carpentry so that Ajayi would have a way of making a living; others taught him reading and writing and, most beautiful of all to Ajayi, the new religion of Christianity. As soon as he could spell out his letters, the youth borrowed a coin from a fellow Yoruba and rushed to buy his first reader. In the long evenings, as the earthenware lamp flickered, Ajayi bent over his book, drinking in each word, each idea. Sometimes he stole a glance at the young girl who often shared his studies. She was Asano, a Yoruba like himself who had been snatched into slavery by raiders and then freed by a British ship. But the two young people did not often joke together or chat lightly. The experiences they had been through, wrenched from their families and carefree village days, had made them serious and mature. Gravely they worked at their lessons, their thoughts turning often toward a future in which, somehow, they would be able to bring to their own people the benefits of what they were learning from the missionaries.

Progressing faster than any of his schoolmates, Ajayi was reading the New Testament within six months after starting school. His eager mind absorbed each verse of the Scriptures. The holy writings became part of him so deeply that he and his teachers soon knew that he was ready to enter the church. On December 11, 1825, he was baptized into his new religion as Samuel Ajayi Crowther, a name given in honor of a far-off member of the committee of the Church Missionary Society. The Reverend Samuel Crowther, vicar of Christ Church in Newgate Street in London, had taken an intense interest in news from Bathurst of Ajayi's progress. It seemed to young Samuel a special omen of a happy future that he had received the name of this good man.

A totally unexpected happiness soon followed. "Samuel, there is something I should like to tell you," said Mr. Davey, his missionary friend and teacher. "Mrs. Davey and I are returning to England. We have thought much about your future, and we know that you cannot go further with your education here in Bathurst. It is our desire to take you with us to England, so that you can continue in the path of learning."

Joy made Samuel stammer as he tried to answer. "I cannot speak to tell you what is in my heart. You and Mrs. Davey are the kindest friends anyone could ever imagine. Thank you! Thank you!"

The flurry of preparations for the trip made the days speed by. Only the thought of leaving Asano made Samuel sad, but she promised to write him all the news about herself and life at Bathurst. Before he had fully realized it, he and the Daveys were aboard ship. Sailing week after week over the calm blue ocean, Samuel could scarcely contain his impatience. What would England look like? How would he be received in this strange land? Would he be able to succeed in an English school as he had at Bathurst? Anxiously he observed and listened to all the passengers on board ship, hoping to learn all he could about the days that lay ahead.

Often he thought of the *Esperanza Felix*, and his heart was full of pain when he thought of the innumerable slaves who had not had the good fortune to be rescued. As he prayed for his brothers in slavery, Samuel knew that his own freedom must serve a purpose. He would dedicate himself to one goal, the ending of slavery; he would spend his life trying to prevent anyone else from having to suffer the anguish he himself had known.

On the coach trip from Portsmouth to London, Samuel's head swam with a kaleidoscope of impressions. The gentle English countryside, with its cultivated fields and neat cottages, was very different from the exuberant jungle foliage and thatched-roof villages of Sierra Leone. The English sun was a pale imitation of the tropical brilliance of the African sun, and Samuel shivered in the chilly breezes. In London, he was amazed by the crowded city streets, the busy shops, the brick factories belching smoke, the cries of hawkers, the carriages drawn by fine horses, the sooty faces of chimney sweeps. At the church school in Liverpool Road, he settled into a busy routine. His schoolwork was strict and demanding, leaving him little time for skylarking. He was often startled and sometimes secretly amused by the attention he received from the other students—English children, to whom the black Yoruba boy was a completely new and never-ending source of fascination.

Samuel lived at the home of the Reverend E. Bickersteth, a secretary of the Church Missionary Society with a large brood of children. English family life, which he was coming to know so well, seemed very pleasant to Samuel—but it was no substitute for a family life of his own. His thoughts turned more and more often to Africa. My own father and mother and brothers and sisters are lost forever, Samuel mused. It is time for me to seek a home and family for myself. Perhaps Asano . . .

After eight months in school, Samuel returned to Sierra Leone in 1827. The colonial government took an immediate interest in this educated young African, eager to work with his own people. He was appointed an assistant schoolmaster, at a salary of £1 ($5) a month. He had scarcely become accustomed to his new position and responsibilities before word came that English missionaries were about to open a new institute for the training of Africans (later called Fourah Bay College), and that Samuel was invited to be their first student. It was a wrench for him to give up his first real job, but young Crowther knew that he must not neglect any opportunity to further his education. The more he could learn, the more he would be able to serve his people and his God.

When Samuel arrived at the institute, he carried with him the large, comfortable mattress he had brought back from England. Mr. Haensel, the principal, sent for his new student at once.

"It is with pleasure, Samuel, that I welcome you as the first of the many students who, we hope, will learn wisdom and godliness at the institute. You have been described as a lad of uncommon ability and steady conduct, with a thirst for knowledge and indefatigable industry. How, then, have you permitted yourself to fall prey to the temptation of luxury?"

"Sir," replied Samuel, "I thank you for your welcome and kindly view of me, which I hope to deserve. As to luxury, it has ever been my object to resist any such desire. What have I done to indicate otherwise?"

"The mattress, my boy. I wish to see you, for the good of your own soul, in that state of lowliness of mind which Africans so easily lose by visits to England. The mattress is indeed a luxury which you must resist. It cannot be used here."

The mattress did not seem to Samuel a threat to a proper state of mind, but he had no choice. Regretfully, with a rebellious murmur inaudible to Mr. Haensel, he removed the precious object. Perhaps it would, in fact, have been too great a luxury for a student at the institute, since the young men who soon came to join Samuel at the school led a modest life with little in the way of comforts. Even Mr. Haensel, with his strict ideas, could find no fault with their simple style of living.

School was, as always, a joy to Samuel. Now that his education was nearing completion and he felt that his future as a schoolmaster would be assured, Samuel thought more and more often of Asano. She, too, had adopted Christianity, and had been baptized Susan Thompson. Like him, she had been educated and was serving as a schoolmistress in Sierra Leone. With beating heart, Samuel approached the governing body of the mission to ask their consent to his marriage. Having received permission, he raced to Susan's side to ask her to become his wife. The two young people, deeply in love, entered into a marriage which led to some fifty years of happy companionship. The three daughters born to them all grew up to marry African clergymen; one son, Dandeson Coates Crowther, became an archdeacon, and the other two, Samuel and Josiah, became prosperous businessmen.

After his wedding and his graduation from Fourah Bay College, Samuel returned to teaching school. In 1834, he was invited to become a member of the staff of the college, where he applied himself vigorously not only to teaching his African students but also to learning Greek and Latin. Caring for his growing family as well as his students, somehow Samuel still found time to squeeze in further reading on his own. The days scarcely seemed long enough for all he wanted to do—training Africans, two of whom later became government chaplains; holding Sunday school in the rickety old Gibraltar Chapel; playing with and teaching his own children;

practicing his religious devotions and struggling with his Greek and Latin; wondering, during restless hours when sleep evaded him, how he could find ways of helping his own people to reach a better life.

Crowther unburdened his troubled thoughts to a white friend, John Bowen, the administrator of a British government office in Freetown. "I am discouraged," Crowther said, "by how far we still have to go. Slavery has not yet been wiped out. My people suffer from terrible diseases and insufficient food. And many still cling to their old pagan ways."

"Samuel, you are not alone in your concerns," his friend sympathized. "There are many Englishmen here in Africa and back in London who share your complaints. In fact, some news has just arrived that might cheer you up." He pulled a newspaper out of his pocket and gave it to Crowther. The African read carefully through the statistics, which showed the tripled growth of West African trade with England in the preceding twenty years. The possibility of even greater growth in profits from African tropical products, continued the article, had stirred the imagination of businessmen and British government officials. To this ferment was added the encouragement of religious societies to "arrest the Foreign Slave-trade at its source."

The newspaper quoted Colonial Secretary Lord John Russell: "It is proposed to establish new commercial relations with those African Chiefs or Powers, within whose dominions the internal Slave-trade of Africa is carried on. . . . To this end, the Queen has directed her Ministers to negotiate conventions or agreements with those Chiefs and Powers." Lord Russell then went on to propose the establishment of British trading posts, "in the hope that the Natives may be taught that there are methods of employing the population more profitable . . . than that of converting them into slaves."

When he came to the end of the article, Crowther looked up and smiled. Bowen began to speak quickly, but in guarded tones.

"Keep this to yourself, Samuel, but in today's mail boat we

received some dispatches that are more up to date than the news-paper. There is going to be a big government expedition up the Niger River. Three steamers of the Royal Navy, the *Albert*, the *Soudan* and the *Wilberforce*, along with the schooner *Amelia*, are being outfitted and will arrive sometime next year."

As Bowen and Crowther eagerly examined the possibilities and problems of the proposed Niger expedition, a similar conversation was taking place thousands of miles away at a meeting of the Church Missionary Society in London. "This is an extraordinary opportunity," pointed out Mr. Dunlop, one of those at the meeting, "for us to do God's work. We have no stations along the Niger River, and no possibility of entering this unknown country by ourselves. I recommend that we ask permission of the government to send two representatives on the expedition, who will try to persuade the local chiefs that a church mission should be established."

"Out of the question. It is too difficult, too dangerous for white men to penetrate the interior. I cannot conceive what the government can be thinking of with this expedition! God's servants must live to do His work, not perish in the fever swamps. We all know the terrible loss of life in Sierra Leone. It will be even worse on the Niger."

"God's servants are not cowards," sternly replied another. "Think of the souls of His children, and overcome your fears."

Yet another voice interrupted the controversy, that of a highly respected minister known for his interest in the society's African activities. "There is indeed a way for our purpose to be accomplished. The Reverend James Frederick Schön, our missionary for 10 years in Sierra Leone, has dedicated himself to the spiritual needs of God's African children. He is a student of African languages, and a brave man as well. He will surely wish to undertake the journey. And why should he not be accompanied by Samuel Crowther, whose work at Fourah Bay College is well-known to all of us?"

"Of course!" exclaimed another voice. "Crowther is the obvious choice. He knows native languages and customs; he is a deeply religious man full of concern for the welfare of his people."

"But he is black! How can we entrust him with this work? We cannot be represented by a black man!"

There was a moment's startled silence, and then a babble of voices as the members responded. Mr. Dunlop raised his hand in admonition, and then spoke to the group. "God knows His children not by the color of their skins but by their devotion to His cause. We should be proud to have Crowther represent us!"

The news of his appointment to the expedition reached Samuel as he sat in his small study with Susan one quiet evening. The flames of the oil lamps cast weird shadows on the walls, reminding Samuel of the hours he and Susan had sat studying together years before. He smiled at her lovingly before opening his letter. Then, with a cry of astonishment, he read the letter out loud.

"What must I do?" he asked when he had finished. "I feel the voice of God calling me in this letter, yet I do not wish to part from you and our children. A family needs a husband and father. Where does my duty lie?"

Gently Susan said, "Do not fear for me and the children. Our good friends here at Fourah Bay will help care for us. You must heed God's word."

"The mighty rivers of our land can become roads to peace, to goodwill among men. They can carry the message of our Lord deep into the hearts of men. Susan, the Niger flows through Yorubaland, where perhaps I can find my own people again. Yes, you are right. I leave you and the children in God's care, and there is no better."

Boarding the *Soudan* at Freetown on July 1, 1841, Samuel settled himself and his few belongings for the voyage. He planned to keep careful notes of the trip in his journal, and the Reverend Schön, on the *Albert*, made similar preparations. They conferred with the twelve Africans Captain Trotter of the *Albert* had hired to act as interpreters. Among them they could handle conversations in Ibo, Kakanda, Bornoa, Laruba, Filatah, Eggarra, Yoruba and

Hausa. However, they knew they would meet many people along the way who spoke other tongues, and they worried about the problem of communicating without a common language. Even today in Nigeria, a country only somewhat larger than Washington, Oregon and California combined, some 250 different languages are spoken.

The expedition set sail on July 3, stopping at Monrovia on July 5 and then pausing now and again along the coast to get firewood. The water was rough, and both men suffered from violent seasickness. The Reverend Schön had to lay aside the Hausa translations on which he was working, and Crowther could barely manage a few moments on his Yoruba vocabulary.

Arriving at Accra, with its English, Dutch and Danish settlements, the ships reprovisioned before continuing their journey. Crowther and Schön went together to look at the glistening white Elmina Castle, which the Portuguese had built in 1481. Its shadowed halls had once echoed to the sound of Columbus' footsteps—and to the shrieking of captives about to be auctioned off as slaves. Shuddering, the men spoke of the horrors within the castle courtyard.

Meditating on the castle's infamous past, Crowther fell silent. Then he spoke decisively: "It is my solemn vow to spend my life in combat against these evils. No child must be snatched from his mother's arms, no husband and wife rent asunder. All people must walk free, all are Our Lord's dear children and servants. I pray for God's help in wiping out forever the unspeakable wickedness of slavery."

In mid-August, the ships entered the river Nun, one of the many mouths of the Niger. As they traveled upstream, they passed native villages. The Reverend Schön knew that white men had been there before because, as he unhappily observed, "the first thing which the natives usually ask for is their favorite rum."

As the expedition continued upstream from the delta and came into the Niger River itself, the swampy, steaming jungle began to change, and the mangroves yielded to forests thick with palm and bamboo trees. From shore, as Samuel noted in his journal, could be seen "large cotton trees of curious shapes." And by August 22, sailing up the Benue on the *Wilberforce*, Schön wrote: "We are now convinced, from the unanimous testimony of the people, that we are the first Europeans, at least within their memory, that ever navigated this branch of the river."

As the *Wilberforce* proceeded through Ibo territory, stopping at the various villages, the expedition found sharp testimony that the slave trade still flourished. At one stop, the Ibo villagers brought a group of nine- or ten-year-old boys to the ship and offered them for sale; all of these children were Yorubas, obviously seized during a raid. Neither the pleas of the explorers nor the urgings of Schön and Crowther availed to secure the freedom of the children. Ruefully thinking of his vow to wipe out slavery, Samuel knew that he would have to redouble his efforts. The end was not yet in sight.

At Ibo, where the Obi (king) sent a gift of a bullock and two hundred yams to welcome the expedition, the first order of business was to discuss the elimination of the slave trade and the possibility of establishing a mission. The Obi would not commit himself, although he expressed interest in these new ideas. "You ask me," the king remarked, "to sell elephant tusks instead of men. But it is far easier to catch a man than an elephant. I must consider the ancient ways of my people and the sacred wishes of our ancestors." The words of the white men impressed the Obi, but what astonished him most of all was that one of the interpreters, Simon Jonas, could read and write. "It is a marvel that a black man, an Ibo man, a slave in times past, should know these wonderful things too!" he exclaimed. He insisted that Simon stay with him until the expedition returned from upriver, slyly suggesting that he could learn much about the proposed new ideas from such a remarkable fellow Ibo.

So far, the expedition had been a success. Relations were being established with various rulers, and the journals of members of the party were full of new and useful information. But a serious blow fell, one which turned the apparent success into a bleak failure. On September 5 the first inkling of misfortune came when several cases of illness broke out on the *Albert* and the *Soudan*. Recognizing the malarial fever, the officers immediately took the usual precautions. The fever was thought to result from poisonous air rising at night from the swamps, so every effort was bent on keeping the men out of the night air. To avoid breathing the poison, the crew stayed below in their cramped quarters, or wrapped themselves from head to toe when they had to work on deck. In the tropical climate of the Niger region, nothing could have been worse for their health. By the 16th of September, forty-seven Europeans, two West Indians and one East Indian lay ill. Death had suddenly become a commonplace. When the ships tried to stop for supplies, the villagers, terrified of the sickness, fought them off with clubs and spears. There was no hope of going on. One by one, the ships, with their cargo of sick and dying men, were forced to return to the coast.

What had been accomplished on this valiant and ill-fated voyage? The Obi of Ibo, as well as the Attah of Eggarra, had finally decided to sign a treaty abolishing the slave trade and setting aside land where future church missions could be established. Much had been learned of the peoples and the geography of the Niger area. But the cost had been too great. Of 145 Europeans on the expedition, forty-eight had been lost in two months. The blight of sickness or death had left only Samuel Crowther untouched. When news of the tragic events reached England, public opinion was outraged by the seeming waste of human life. Not for twelve long years would it be possible to overcome the fear of another disaster and plan a new Niger expedition.

Both Crowther and the Reverend Schön, reporting to the Church Missionary Society on their experiences, had reached one major conclusion: white men could not carry on the future mission work needed on the Niger. "I am reluctantly led to adopt the opinion," Samuel wrote, "that Africa can be chiefly benefited by her own children." Mr. Schön went further: he reported that whatever good relations had been established with the African rulers had resulted from the patience, tact and skill of Samuel Crowther. "I believe," said Schön, "that native Africans should be ordained as ministers, to carry the gospel message to their own people. This expedition may have failed, but Crowther at least has succeeded in a very special way. He has taught us that black Africans are certainly our equals—nay, our superiors—at this kind of work."

Once persuaded, the society acted quickly. They invited Crowther to return to England to attend the society's college at Islington, where he could study for the ministry. There were more than a few skeptics who doubted the black man's ability to pass the rigorous course of study, but he amazed both his teachers and associates by his ability to learn quickly and deeply. The last doubters were silenced by the report of the Bishop's examiners: "His papers were capital, and his Latin remarkably good." On Trinity Sunday, June 11, 1843, Samuel received his deacon's order, and in October of that year he was ordained a minister, the first black man to take holy orders under the Church Missionary Society.

Two months after Crowther became a minister, he was back in Africa. A huge crowd gathered on Sunday in the Mission Church in Freetown. Some were Christians, but others had come only out of curiosity. "Is it really true," they whispered to one another, "that an African, a Yoruba, will preach today?" "As Allah wills," muttered a Mohammedan who had joined the waiting throng. Breathlessly, the people watched the door through which the minister would enter—and there, for all to see, came the black-robed Reverend Samuel Ajayi Crowther, mounting the pulpit in solemn dignity as a sigh of wonder swept through the room. Even those who understood no English listened in silent concentration as the sermon began.

But neither the fact that Crowther was black nor that he soon began to preach in Yoruba so that more people could understand his sermons saved the minister from bitter opposition. Some Africans felt betrayed by Crowther's adoption of the white man's religion. Others, especially those who faithfully worshiped Shango, the god of thunder, were horrified that their own gods were under attack. They fiercely rejected Samuel's attempts to explain electricity and how thunder and lightning were caused. "How I wish," exclaimed Crowther, "that I had an electrical machine with which to teach! Then indeed would the people begin to accept scientific principles instead of superstition."

Samuel's efforts to bring learning to Sierra Leone extended far beyond the preaching of sermons in his native language. He also undertook the translation of the gospels into Yoruba, and continued to work on his vocabulary of the Yoruba tongue. Later, Oxford University was to name him an honorary Doctor of Divinity because of his outstanding literary accomplishments—his translations and his grammar and dictionary of Yoruba.

News began to arrive at Freetown that, many miles away, Yoruba tribesmen fleeing from Fulani raids had started a new settlement. Taking shelter under the Olumo rock just off the river Ogun in Yorubaland, the refugees named their new village Abeokuta ("Under the Stone"). From travelers Crowther learned that no white man had ever visited the town, and Christianity was unknown. A few liberated Yoruba slaves undertook the journey to Abeokuta and, when word trickled back that all was well, many prepared to leave Sierra Leone to rejoin their kinsmen. It was with dismay that the Christian ministers of Sierra Leone realized that their converts, with no mission to offer religious services in Abeokuta, would probably relapse from Christianity. The Reverend Crowther, concerned about this possibility, had another reason, too, for urging the establishment of a new church mission at Abeokuta. He and his family would be able to return to Yorubaland after his many years of separation from his own people. God willing, he might even be able to discover some of his long-lost relatives and childhood friends.

Chief Sodeke of Abeokuta responded to an inquiry by issuing a friendly invitation to the missionaries, and plans for the journey were quickly readied. But Sodeke's death, followed by a period of turmoil in Abeokuta, delayed the arrival of the missionary party. It was months later, after a weary period of waiting in Badagry, that the missionaries were able to enter Abeokuta under the protection of the new chief, Sagbue. The tropical downpour which soaked the skins of the Crowther family and of the Reverend Townsend (the first white man to see the town) did not dampen their spirits. They were exhilarated by the welcome which awaited them. Arrayed in a brilliantly striped cloak, the town crier shook his monkey-skin headdress as he clanged the bell he held in one hand and waved an ax in the other, telling the people of Abeokuta to offer the chief's honored guests the hospitality due a returning kinsman.

Not long after his arrival in Abeokuta, Crowther stood talking on the street one day to a small group of Africans. He was telling them the story of his life, and slowly the group grew as other villagers stopped to listen. Ajayi, Oshogun, Fulani raid—the words fell on the quiet air as Samuel talked of his past. Suddenly there was a commotion as a short, elderly man pushed his way forward and fell on Crowther's neck. "I am your uncle, Ajayi, the brother of your mother!" Tears pricked Samuel's eyelids as his uncle embraced him and revealed that his mother and sisters, whom he had not seen in a quarter of a century, were still alive in the neighboring town of Abaka. Together Samuel and his uncle rushed to tell the joyous news to Susan. With sorrow Samuel heard the tale of his mother's experiences—she had been sold in the market as a household slave, and after a second sale she had remained in slavery while her daughter worked to save enough cowrie shells to buy her mother's freedom. A year's pay, some £ 4.10 (about $20) had earned her liberation. Since Crowther could not leave his work at Abeokuta, he immediately sent word for his family to join him.

The news that Samuel was alive fell on unbelieving ears when it reached his sisters. They could not credit such a fantastic tale, nor would they come to Abeokuta to see for themselves. But his mother and half-brother, although they trembled with fear of a possible disappointment, decided to take the risk. Samuel later described the touching reunion. "When my mother saw me, she trembled. She could not believe her own eyes. We grasped one another, looking at one another in silence and great astonishment, while the big tears rolled down her emaciated cheeks. . . . We could not say much, but sat still, casting many an affectionate look towards each other, an affection which twenty-five years' separation had not extinguished. I cannot describe my feelings. I had given up all hope, and now . . . we were brought together again."

The silence did not last for long. There was so much to tell! Samuel's mother embraced Susan and was delighted with her new-found grandchildren. The old lady marveled at her son's accomplishments and kept urging him to tell her more about his remarkable life.

After this joyful reunion, Samuel's mother decided to live in Abeokuta, where she became the Reverend Crowther's first Christian convert. As he pronounced his mother's new Christian name, Hannah, Crowther added a prayer of his own: "God has been so good to me. May I carry His goodness to all of my people."

Samuel's sisters, whom he had visited in Abaka, were soon to have proof of his desire to help others. Egba warriors, seeking slaves, came to Abaka and laid siege to the town. When it was forced to surrender after several months, the townspeople were seized and taken to Abeokuta to be sold. Among the tragic group of prisoners, Samuel recognized his brother, his two sisters and their children. Had he had the money, he would have ransomed all the slaves, but his savings totaled only £ 30. With this he was at least able to purchase the freedom of his relatives.

When the next invitation came for Crowther to visit England in 1851, it was as the chief expert on the Niger area that he arrived in London. Discussing the geography, tribal life and future commercial development of the region with British Foreign Secretary Lord Palmerston, Samuel emphasized the continuing horror of the slave trade. The king of Dahomey and the king of Lagos were in large measure responsible, Samuel insisted, as he urged Lord Palmerston to move even more strongly against slavery.

Sandwiched in between his official activities, Samuel took what time he could to go sightseeing with Susan in London. Constantly busy, he met many people—anyone who could possibly be helpful in improving the life of the West Africans. When he spoke to the students at Cambridge University, he pleaded with them to consider a life as missionaries in Africa. With the Church Missionary Society, he stressed the needs of the people of his region. At night, he and Susan quietly discussed their hopes for the Niger area.

It was with high excitement that Samuel returned to Susan one day to describe his interview with Queen Victoria, who had herself requested that he visit her. "When I came to Windsor Castle, Susan, I was conducted to an upper drawing room, where I chatted with Prince Albert. I did not know who the simply dressed little lady was, since she remained at first in the background. When I was presented to the Queen, I trembled from head to foot, and could not open my mouth to answer the questions that followed."

"What did you talk about, Samuel?"

"Her Majesty asked me to explain the conditions of the Niger, and I told her much of the region, using a map to make things clear. She was truly interested, and questioned me deeply on the slave trade. I told her that if King Kasoko of Lagos could be brought under control, that part of the coast would see the end of slavery!"

Susan smiled tenderly as Crowther continued to describe the meeting. How fortunate, she thought, that the Queen had been able to learn about the Niger from Samuel, for who else could give as clear and true a picture? Then Susan realized, with a start, that her husband had stopped talking and was regarding her with an expectant air.

"What else happened?" she asked.

"Her Majesty asked me to recite the Lord's Prayer in Yoruba, for she wished to hear the language. When I had finished, she thanked me and said that Yoruba was a sweet and melodious tongue."

Samuel was charmed by his meeting with the Queen, but a greater happiness came most unexpectedly. Working on his translations at Church Missionary House in Salisbury Square, Crowther raised his head now and then to glance out of the window. He stared unseeingly at the passers-by, but suddenly his attention was riveted on an elderly man who was approaching. Incredulous, Crowther sprang to his feet and rushed out to take a better look. Yes, there could be no doubt—it was indeed Captain (now Sir) Henry Leeke of the *Myrmidon*, who had saved young Ajayi from slavery thirty years before! When he made himself known to Sir Henry, the two men could not contain their joy and surprise, Sir Henry exclaiming over and over again, "But is it really you! How wonderful!" On the spot, the two agreed that the Crowthers would visit Sir Henry at his house in Kent. When they did so, the village assembled in their church to hear the former slave boy preach on the divine goodness and guidance which had reunited him with his rescuer.

Soon after he returned to Africa in June of 1852, the Reverend Crowther was again invited to go on a Niger expedition, the first since the ill-fated trip of 1841. This second expedition was organized by a London merchant, MacGregor Laird, who dreamed of the vast profits which could come from increased trade with the Niger region. On this journey, which penetrated the Niger 250 miles deeper than any earlier exploration, one of the great successes lay in the good health of the expedition. During the four months that were spent on the river, not a single person of the twelve Europeans and fifty-four Africans died or even became sick—and all because Dr. J. Baikie, who accompanied the expedition to make geographic observations, gave each person five grains of quinine daily. Malaria, the great killer of 1841, had lost its threat.

Crowther readied himself for this second journey into the interior by planning carefully how to carry out his chief interests. "It is the good hand of the Lord which is evidently beckoning us forward in our efforts to reach these long-isolated members of the human family and to bring them within the circle of Christian civilization," Samuel said to Susan as he described his plans for the expedition.

"We will miss you, Samuel," she sighed, "but you must indeed help establish God's kingdom among our people and seek to bring them a better life."

"One way," replied Crowther, "to do God's work is to bring new ways of making a living to the people. Trade in goods is morally superior to trade in men, but our people must also learn that they can prosper more by selling cotton and lumber and ivory instead of human flesh."

"But how can you show them?"

"I am taking seven hundredweight of clean cotton to Lagos with me to be shipped to Manchester. I also will show the farmers of the Niger how to use the cotton gin, so they may be able to clean the fiber quickly and easily. May this be the beginning of a new and healthy commerce, both for England and for us!"

The efforts of Crowther and others bore fruit: in 1851, Abeokuta exported 235 pounds of cotton to England; by 1859, the amount stood at 6,000 bales, or 720,000 pounds.

Laird's *Pleiad*, with Crowther aboard, sailed from Fernando Po on July 8, 1854. "About 9 p.m. we weighed for the Nun, with two large iron canoes laden with coals in tow; the friends who accompanied us a short distance from the harbor left us with hearty cheers. As the wind rose, and the swell became heavy, the canoes did not tow well, and there was some fear of their being upset: the night was, therefore, passed with some anxiety."

As the fuel canoes continued to labor from the heavy swells and strong current, pouring rains added to the *Pleiad*'s difficulties. The high surf rocked the steamer and, in the misery of his seasickness, Samuel wondered wildly whether this expedition was destined to be as unhappy as that of 1841. But somehow each obstacle was overcome—the breaking of the spindle of the ship's safety valve, the tearing of the hawser of one of the canoes, the running aground of the *Pleiad* when the wrong channel was followed— and by July 16, Crowther was able to turn his attention to the region through which the ship was now passing. Traces of cultivation were beginning to appear along the river banks, and Crowther observed that the shores looked very different from 1841, with many newly cleared areas among the lofty palm trees.

The slave trade, although diminished, had by no means come to a

halt. At many points in the journey, Crowther was heartsick at
what he saw. In one area, near the confluence of the Niger and the
Benue Rivers, there was scarcely a village to be seen on the right
bank of the river, while the left bank was dotted with numerous
little towns. The desolation of the right bank was a silent witness
to a series of raids by a chieftain named Dasaba, in which some
hundred towns and villages had been destroyed.

The slave trade and the tribal warfare that nourished it, Samuel
thought, might help account for the hostility toward Europeans
which the expedition so often encountered. Some villages greeted
the ship by waving a white cloth as a sign of peace. In these
friendly regions as many as 1,000 people would gather in the
marketplace to hear Crowther preach his message of love and
goodwill. But in other areas, warriors met them with "bows bent
and poisoned arrows ready for action." Some of these hostile groups
thought the strangers were slave raiders and sought to protect
their villages; others sought to protect their income from the slave
trade and had been forewarned by other slavers about the dangerous intentions of the black minister. Crowther warned Captain
Taylor and Dr. Hutchinson, "Do not press our visits too quickly
on those who distrust us. It is not easy for the people to overcome
their suspicion of strangers. We must move slowly and always with
kindness and gifts."

Sometimes a ruler, already friendly, met the expedition with a
gala greeting. The band of drummers and a fifer sent by the Attah
of Idda shook the treetops with their playing. Otí, the Attah's
messenger, spun wildly in his dance of welcome, flinging his sword
into the air and skillfully catching it in flight. On the two-mile
zigzag walk to the Attah's palace, friendly faces peered out from
the low doorways and porches. The Attah himself, resplendent in
a silk-velvet robe and a crown of white beads fringed with red
parrot tails in front, fingered the strings of cowries and coral beads
around his neck as he poured out phrases of greeting and friendship. One of the Attah's men, who spoke Hausa, translated the
words of the Igára language, to be interpreted in turn into Yoruba

by Crowther's aide, Aliheli. A pot of honey was placed before the
delegation from the *Pleiad*, and around it calabashes of fresh milk
and butter. The Attah and his assembled people listened carefully
to Crowther's message, but they were in no hurry to make up
their minds about any of his proposals. The chief smilingly pointed
out, "A new chicken, when brought into the yard, walks gently
and looks steadily on the old ones to see what they do."

When he later described the expedition to his eager family,
Crowther was able to report some personal successes. He told his
wife and children of seeds of thought he had planted in the sermons he had preached and the plans for the opening of many
new missions. Too, some traders had been willing to recognize
that there was greater prosperity in cotton, palm oil and ivory
than in the slave trade. And lastly he showed them his notebooks,
full of curious scribbles, in which he had jotted down the strange
words of many languages for use in future grammars or dictionaries.

Crowther's devotion to his work and his people had by now
become a by-word in the Church Missionary Society back in England. It was clear that Crowther was a mainstay of the society's
efforts in West Africa. When another expedition was planned in
1857, the society commissioned the Reverend Crowther to found
its new Niger Mission. He was to be accompanied by the Reverend
J. C. Taylor, an Ibo born in Sierra Leone whose father and mother,
like Crowther, were liberated slaves. The mission was planned almost entirely as an African project, to be staffed by black Christians—a notable exception to most missionary work in Africa at
that time, and a tribute to the labors of Crowther and the other
black ministers who had followed him in the Niger region.

As he left Fernando Po for the new voyage in 1857, Samuel had
no thought that this trip, whose goal was the towns of Kano, Rabbah
and Sokoto in the Mohammedan Fulani kingdom, would keep him
away from home and family for two and a half years. But the
Dayspring, sturdy vessel though she was, ran aground on a hidden
rock in December of 1857 and had to be abandoned. The local
villagers were certain that Ketsa, the spirit of the holy rock, had

taken revenge on those who dared to invade his domain. The explorers, unable to go further, returned to Rabbah by canoe to wait until another ship could come for them. But Crowther was not one to let the time pass in worry or idleness. Using the five circular huts the shipwrecked voyagers had built at Rabbah as his headquarters, he traveled from village to village, preaching, studying the people and their languages, laying the groundwork for missions to be established and urging the Africans to grow products for trade with the Europeans. The messenger of a Nupe chief, Usuman Zaki, had been sent to Rabbah to inquire about the purposes of the *Dayspring* expedition. Crowther wanted to illustrate his concern for the future progress of Africa. "Pointing to a cotton gin, I said, 'this is our gun'; to the clean cotton puffing out of it, 'that is our powder'; to the cowries that are the proceeds of the operation, 'there are the shots which England, the friend of Africa, desires that she should receive.' "

In this way Crowther spent more than a year before the stranded expedition was picked up by the rescue ship *Sunbeam*. Undaunted by previous difficulties, the Reverend Crowther again sailed up the Niger River during the summer of 1859, this time on the *Rainbow*. Finding the passage blocked at the confluence, where the Benue flows into the Niger, the ship could go no further. As she returned downriver, the *Rainbow* was fired on from shore and two men were killed. This sad event so infuriated the British that they closed the Niger for two years, and the Reverend Crowther was unable to supervise the mission stations he had established.

In July of 1861, HMS *Espoir* sailed upstream to seek revenge against the villages from which the firing had come. Crowther wangled passage so that he could visit the religious outposts cut off by the shutdown of the river. Thus he stood on deck when the *Espoir* began shelling the hostile villages. As he watched his fellow Africans fall under the hail of British bullets, Samuel shuddered. His eyes wet with tears, he turned away, his heart rebelling at the thought that death should come thus to the very people whom he had vowed to protect from the evils of slavery and superstition. Trembling, he searched for an answer, praying that God would help him accept the awful necessity of what was happening. He deeply believed that Christianity and European ways of living could help the African people, but he was torn with anguish that the price for this advancement should be so high.

Samuel tried to put the episode aside, in his strong belief that any barrier to the English and to the Church was also a barrier to progress for his countrymen. He also had much else to think about. The Church Missionary Society had begun to recognize that it was not enough to have only one bishop in West Africa. The Bishop of Sierra Leone, almost 2,000 miles from the Niger region, could not possibly supervise the society's work in Lagos, Abeokuta, Onitsha, Gbebe and other parts of the area. Why not have a bishop of the Niger? And who could possibly be a better choice than Samuel Ajayi Crowther? He knew the Niger intimately, he had been a leader in establishing the numerous missions, his own city of Abeokuta had grown by leaps and bounds, he was a profound student of religion and he was respected by white and black alike. The choice was clear.

With the approval of the Archbishop of Canterbury, a royal license was issued for "Our truly and well-beloved Samuel Ajayi Crowther, Clerk in Holy Orders, to be a Bishop of the Church of England in the West African territories beyond the British dominions." On the 29th of June, 1864, in Canterbury Cathedral, the former slave boy, amid solemn pomp and ceremony, was consecrated Bishop of the Niger Territories. The Archbishop of Canterbury, attended by five other bishops, performed the ritual. So great was the excitement in England that special trains were run from London to Canterbury for the event, and the cathedral bulged with the press of fascinated spectators. In places of honor sat Admiral Sir Henry Leeke, former captain of the *Myrmidon*, and Mrs. Weeks, one of Samuel's early friends and teachers in Sierra Leone.

Soon back at the Niger, Bishop Crowther continued his lifetime work of preaching, traveling, supervising the missions, fighting against the slave trade, training native Africans for mission work and spurring the growth of trade and prosperity. He concentrated mainly on the Niger Delta, where the twenty-six mouths of the river, fanning out from 140 miles inland, spread over 120 miles, from Lagos to Old Calabar. He was dismayed by the opposition of some of the native priests, who tried to preserve the old gods and tribal rituals. Often they persecuted the Christian converts. At Bonny, where the easternmost mouth of the Niger winds sluggishly through mangrove thickets into the sea, the fiery chants of the witch doctors whipped the people into a frenzy of hatred. They drove the Christians into the wilderness, where, stripped naked, they were pinned to the ground to die of starvation while the mosquitoes, sandflies and driver ants feasted on their tormented bodies. It took three years of concentrated effort by Bishop Crowther's missionaries to gain freedom of worship for the Christians at Bonny. On a triumphant note of thanksgiving, the missionaries reported to their bishop that the head chief of Bonny had been baptized; during the great celebration that followed, two boatloads of idols had been dumped into the river.

From time to time Bishop Crowther called together the heads of the far-flung mission stations to confer on their many problems. "We know that Africa needs both the gospel and the plow," he said in his opening address at one meeting, "both Christianity and industry. These two words are worthy to be written in letters of gold and preserved in a casket of silver! In our years of hopes and fears, the Lord has helped us. But we must now take a searching look at where we stand and carefully examine our plans for the future."

An old friend, Elijah Adukesi, began the discussion in somber tones. "I foresee much trouble to come. It has to do with European traders," he explained. "Our people think of the church mission and the trading station as one and the same thing. Wherever there is a mission, white men also come to buy and sell. Of course, that is to our benefit because the traders provide us with transportation and bring our supplies upstream. But when our people are cheated by the white men, they blame us. The traders come and go, but the mission remains in the village as a symbol of the Europeans who take advantage of Africans. We preach that greed is a sin, but in the minds of our people the white man's religion is a cover for greed."

A white agent of the Church Missionary Society rose to agree with the Reverend Adukesi. "Something recently happened to me which helps explain how Africans feel. As you all know, I have just completed an inspection tour of the Niger missions. At one town I took part in the Sunday evening service, and the next day, as I was leaving, the native missionary told me: 'You greatly astonished our people last evening. Though the station has been in existence twenty years, you are the first white man that they or I have heard pray or sing here. We always tell the people that we are sent and supported by good white people in England to teach them the Way of Life. But they, from having seen the white traders busily engaged about their trade, and never attending to or taking part in religious services, have drawn the conclusion that whilst teaching, preaching and worship are part of the white man's religion, trading and getting money must be the most important part of it, and to this, therefore, he attends himself; but that preaching and teaching, and generally the spreading of his religion, being matters of minor importance, he pays black men to attend to for him.' "

Everyone laughed, but sadly concluded that the problem remained.

"On the other hand," the missionary from Onitsha pointed out, "those who come to our stations are losing their fears of their imaginary deities. We have helped to stop the abominable practice of human sacrifice and have often persuaded the kings or chiefs to substitute an animal victim. There has also been more friendly feeling and union among the neighboring tribes since our establishment among them."

"It is true," said one of the other African ministers, "that much good has been done, although much more is needed in a practical

way. We have introduced cassava plants and fruit trees, and taught
the villagers to improve their yams and to raise a second crop of
Indian corn. Now the people have food all year round, instead
of near-starvation during the three months when the old crop was
consumed and the new crop not yet ripe."

"We can be proud," Crowther said, "of what we have accomplished at Lokoja, Idda, Onitsha, Akassa, Bonny and other places.
But our work represents only a beginning, the opening of a door.
The celestial light has shone on some of our brothers, but there is
still much to do. It is only human that some of us become discouraged, but I know that God in His own good time will answer
our humble petitions. We must labor on!"

It was only with his wife that Samuel could express his deepest
fears and doubts. "Perhaps I am not fit to be a bishop," he told
her. "If I were, I would not have so many problems at the mission
stations. Some of my workers have even dipped their fingers into
our funds, and others have taken to drink."

"Are you to blame for human weakness?" she asked consolingly.
"You have always trodden in the path of faith and humbleness.
Nor have you ever closed your eyes to the faults of some of the
agents of the Niger Mission. No one could have labored more
earnestly and diligently than you!"

"There is so much that discourages me," Crowther said painfully.
"Some of our converts take advantage of our mission schooling and
medical care, only to return thereafter to the superstitions of their
forefathers. I cannot even supervise all the stations to ensure their
proper conduct."

"You have always been eager to bring a better life to your
people," Susan answered firmly. "Of course, this has meant a rapid
expansion of the stations. How could you possibly supervise each
one—especially here in this huge territory, with such poor transportation and so few well-trained workers? Do not doubt yourself,
Samuel! I know that God is well pleased with your service to him."

It may be that the doubts, the questions and the knowledge of
failure as well as achievement which touched the bishop's last

years are the mark of every life which has been rich in experience
and effort. Samuel Ajayi Crowther died in Lagos on New Year's
Eve of 1891, and many voices were raised in tribute to his achievements. The historian of the Church Missionary Society, Dr. Eugene
Stock, eulogized: "A kidnaped slave in 1821; a rescued slave in
1822; a mission schoolboy in 1823; a baptized Christian in 1825;
a college student in 1826; a teacher in 1828; a clergyman in 1843;
a missionary to the country whence he had been stolen in 1845; the
founder of a new mission in 1857; the first Negro bishop in 1864—
where is the parallel to such a life?" The little black boy, uprooted
from his village, his family and his religion, had spent his life in
dedicated labor to benefit his people.

A Nigerian broadcaster, speaking a few years ago of outstanding
Nigerians of the 19th century, said: "The life of Ajayi Crowther
. . . is an epic of the anti-slavery movement in West Africa, and
his whole life is illustrative of the redeeming grace of the gospel
message." Emphasizing that most whites at that period thought of
the black man as something less than human, he added that "in
spite of the prejudices against his race at this time . . . Crowther
rose to be a bishop and thereby vindicated Africans as a whole."
He was full of concern for his fellow Africans, eager to demonstrate
not only the path to religious salvation but also ways to improve
their daily lives. Above all, he devoted himself to the total elimination of slavery and the introduction of happier and more profitable
methods of earning a living. Today, Nigerians honor his memory
as a shining example of achievement and love for humanity.

MOSHOESHOE

THE pounding rhythm of the sheepskin drums and the high-pitched melodies of the *lesiba* filled the air over Thaba Bosiu, the Mountain of the Night. Moshoeshoe stared thoughtfully at the dim horizon, scarcely hearing the chant of the medicine men: "Sacred ashes of plants which can withstand the howling winds of winter, sharp needles from the cruel thorn trees to defend us from our enemies, claws of the lion to give us strength and courage, the skin of a snake for wisdom, feathers of a hawk to give our hunters skill, hairs of a bull to promise many children so our tribe may grow. . . ."

The weary journey of the Basotho people to safety had ended. Moshoeshoe, the chieftain, smiled as he gazed around him in the twilight at the tall plateau, circled with sheer rock faces on three sides, accessible only by steep and easily defended trails on the fourth side. Here, he thought, our Bamonageng people, hand in hand with those who have joined us, will build our new Basotho nation. Here we will live at peace. Here our new huts will rise. Our women will dig the holes for pumpkin seeds, calabash and other gourds, melons and beans. Our men will explore the nearby mountains and sheltered valleys for places to grow sorghum and kaffir corn and to pasture our cows, sheep and goats.

The sharp beat of the drums called Moshoeshoe back from his daydreaming, and he sighed with pleasure at the sight of the medicine men blessing the new home. Their faces whitened with clay, and the long tails of their monkey-skin aprons flying, the witch doctors whirled about. Home, Moshoeshoe said to himself exultantly, we are home at last!

Moshoeshoe could not know, as he dreamed of peace and prosperity on that day in 1823, that the newborn Basotho nation would struggle as mightily for safety in the future as it had in the past. He was not aware that some 700 miles to the southwest, in Cape Town, rumblings of discontent were beginning to stir the Boers, descendants of early Dutch pioneers in South Africa, who had recently come under English rule. These hardy white men, whose ancestors had come to South Africa almost 200 years earlier, were preparing to seek new lands to the north, far from the power of

their British governors, and this northward drive would inevitably
bring them into conflict with Moshoeshoe's people.

But of all this, Moshoeshoe knew nothing. His little world, into
which no white man had yet entered, was ringed only by the
threatening tribes which surrounded him. His thoughts slipped
back to the enemies whom he had defeated or outwitted in the
years before the flight to Thaba Bosiu—Ramonaheng, Chaka the
Zulu, the Bafokeng, the Batlokoa, the Matabele. His heart joyous
at the thought that no enemy could attack the fastness of the
Mountain of the Night, Moshoeshoe drained a calabash of home-
brewed beer as he watched the ceremony of blessing.

The dung fires were burning low and, as the women quietly prepared for the night, the voices of the storytellers rose and fell in
the stillness. They spoke of the history of their tribe—how the
Bamonageng, the People of the Crocodile, were once great but
had fallen on evil days, how their enemies had burned and
plundered their villages, how the tribe had been hungry and piti-
fully weak. "It was then" said Moshoeshoe's father, Mokhachane,
"that my son was born. It was the time of the great drought.
Our enemies were powerful, and many of our people died. The
birth of a son should make glad the heart of his father, but not
at that time. There was not enough to eat for our warriors who
protected us. And so we named him Lepoqo, the Trouble, for one
more mouth to feed was indeed trouble, nothing more." Mokhachane
smiled and went on. "As a child he was always full of mischief,
and so he was renamed Thlaputte, the Busy One."

"Then why is he now called Moshoeshoe?" piped the sleepy
voice of one of the little boys still struggling to stay awake.

"He is Moshoeshoe the Barber, who shaved our enemies clean.
As a young warrior, he turned our luck when he raided our enemy
Ramonaheng and shaved him clean of all his cattle." The crowd
chanted over and over, "Mshweshwe, Mshweshwe, Mshweshwe
. . ." and the youngsters suddenly understood that the word for
barber in the Sesotho language imitates the sound of a razor scrap-
ing against the skin—"Mshweshwe, Mshweshwe, Mshweshwe."

"I was proud to be a knife in the heart of our enemies," Moshoeshoe mused, "but that was before I met Mohlomi. My grandfather Peete had long told me stories of my cousin Mohlomi, who went from tribe to tribe preaching not hate and revenge but love and friendship, cooperation, goodwill, tolerance. I had long known Mohlomi's wife and children in our village, but I knew too that Mohlomi had many wives. It was Peete who explained that, each time he visited a new tribe, Mohlomi chose a wife, set up a home and fathered a child before moving on to spread his ideas against war and injustice to one's fellow man. In this way Mohlomi was always assured of a welcome when he returned to the village a few months or a few years later. Our kinsman Mohlomi hoped that when different tribes thought of going to war, his many children scattered everywhere would not want to kill their brothers and would leave in peace."

"Those were murderous times," young Thlotsi said. "How could Mohlomi go unarmed from tribe to tribe?"

"Mohlomi had the gift of healing," Moshoeshoe replied. "He could draw the sickness out of a child without casting spells or throwing the bones. He did not dance or sprinkle magic powders, but he could make the rain. Why should anyone harm such a man?"

Moshoeshoe paused, and his face lit up. "I remember when I first saw Mohlomi. It was three summers after my initiation when grandfather Peete told me our kinsman was visiting nearby. Together we walked toward the mountain Menkhoaneng, and when we entered the village I saw the crowd surrounding a short, fat old man who walked among them, embracing everyone, talking softly. There were many unfamiliar faces in the crowd. If they were not our Bamonageng, why had they traveled from far away to spend just a few hours with Mohlomi? What was the secret of his power?

"Mohlomi noticed us, and came to bless me by brushing his forehead against my own. Then he detached one of his long brass earrings and fastened it in my ear. We drank in turn from the same calabash, and then I appealed to Mohlomi for his help. I wanted the secret of magic for the Bamonageng to gain victory over our enemies."

There was no sound around the dying fires as Moshoeshoe's listeners waited spellbound for him to tell them the secret of Mohlomi's medicine.

"'My son,' Mohlomi answered me, 'power is not acquired by medicine. Medicine magic is in the heart. One day you will rule men, Moshoeshoe. Learn, then, to know them. What does it mean to be a good chief, my son?'

"I answered without hesitation. 'To kill my people's enemies. To bring back many cattle from raids. To protect our tribe from attack.' But when Mohlomi replied, the sadness in his voice told me he did not agree. 'My cousin,' he said, 'I see you are devoted to the People of the Crocodile and would lift them to the pinnacle of power over all other tribes, just as the tallest mountain looks down on all the other mountains. But remember, Moshoeshoe, that the Bamonageng alone are nothing. The Bamonageng with enemies, even if they are conquered and downtrodden enemies, are less than nothing. But the Bamonageng with friends can be a great people.'

"How could I follow such advice? I could not tell my warriors to be friendly with their enemies. I could not go unarmed to the tribes I had raided.

"'No, it is never a light thing to work for peace,' Mohlomi continued, 'but it is better to thresh corn than to sharpen the spear. You are brave, Moshoeshoe, and skillful. You can be victorious. But what is the price of victory? For the new herd of cattle the tribe gains, how many men must lose their lives? How many children must grow up without fathers to guide them? You know our people despise those who are weak and cannot take care of themselves; how will you stop the suffering of the wounded who come back from war with broken bodies? How will your people live with unceasing fear of revenge by your defeated enemies?'

"Our men would be made proud and arrogant by beating down others, I thought. What would I do if they no longer remembered

how they themselves once trembled with fear and began instead to
enslave others? Now I could understand that the ground wet with
the blood of enemies is slippery."

Moshoeshoe sat silent, remembering. Slowly the people drifted
away from the ceremonial circle, and the curling smoke of the dying
fires carried the unspoken memories of the Bamonageng, the People
of the Crocodile, into the black night sky.

After his meeting with Mohlomi, the eighteen-year-old Moshoeshoe soon found an opportunity to test his new ideas. The neighboring Bafokeng, tough, enterprising cattle raiders, were threatening
the very lives of the Bamonageng. Forced to retaliate, Moshoeshoe
struck at the Bafokeng village of Butha-Buthe, killing or scattering
the men and seizing the women, children and cattle. But instead
of enslaving the captured Bafokeng, Moshoeshoe tried a new tack.
He married 'Mamohato, a lovely Bafokeng captive, and with her
help persuaded the Bafokeng survivors who had fled into the mountains to join in peaceful brotherhood with the Bamonageng.

The Bafokeng were the first to join the Bamonageng in building
the Basotho nation, but the pattern was repeated many times.
Moshoeshoe later defeated the Basia and chose his second and
third wives, 'Mamoseketsi and 'Maselometsi, from among the captives. Over the years Moshoeshoe kept an open door for frightened
outcasts, starving refugees fleeing from slavery, murder, cannibalism, former enemies—for anyone who approached in peace and
would work and contribute to his growing nation.

Since the deserted Bafokeng village of Butha-Buthe seemed to
be located in a better defensive position than the Bamonageng
villages, the two united peoples decided to move to Butha-Buthe
and rebuild it. It was there that the news of the Wars of Calamity
reached Moshoeshoe. First there were only rumors, and then a
growing number of terrified refugees. Soon the story emerged
clearly. Over the mountains and near the great ocean a powerful
Zulu chief named Chaka had seized control of a number of tribes.
A ruthless dictator, Chaka had used treachery, murder, torture

and terror to create a war machine which wiped out everyone and everything which stood in his way. His soldiers knew better than to come home defeated; any warrior not victorious in battle was killed by Chaka.

One of these Zulu soldiers fled and found his way over the mountains to Butha-Buthe. He told Moshoeshoe how the Zulu legions would swoop down on a village, kill all the men and old people, gather up any food they could use, burn the huts and the crops and march the women and children off into slavery in Zululand. Moshoeshoe could hardly believe that soldiers were not allowed to marry and have separate families, that all children were brought up in youth camps separated from their fathers and mothers. Everything went toward spreading Zulu domination over a bigger and bigger area, toward making Chaka more and more powerful. And as he grew more powerful, he grew more cruel.

New refugees came staggering into Butha-Buthe one day, emaciated and starving. Their tribe had been fortunate enough to get a warning that Chaka's terrible legions were marching on the *kraals*. A herdboy some miles from their village had spotted the Zulus' night encampment and had abandoned the cattle to run back and sound the alarm. The villagers had immediately fled their homes. As they recalled their terror, tears came to their eyes. They had not had time to take anything with them; they had even left their pots full of mealie porridge cooking on the slow dung fires.

Not all the refugees from Chaka's cruelty came to Butha-Buthe asking for pity and help. Some attacked, and Moshoeshoe's men frequently had to abandon their work to fight off invaders.

There may have been as many as two and a half million people displaced by Chaka, roaming back and forth across the countryside, a hungry, frightened, vicious horde. They were hemmed into a small area by deserts, mountains, swamps and the guns of Boer farmers to the south. In their desperation, they turned on each other. Those few tribes that still held their ground were driven from their home and lands. On being deprived of its source of food, each clan in turn swooped down on some other peaceful *kraal*.

Preoccupied with their struggle for domination of the Cape Province, the Boers and the English took little notice of the turmoil. Only a few whites, isolated missionaries, had contact with the black tribes to the north and east. "Only on occasion did the seething cauldron of humanity fling a spatter of wreckage up over the rim that gave a hint of what was going on in the interior," wrote a historian.

Moshoeshoe's people were among the few who still held their territory in this deadly game of musical chairs, but Moshoeshoe finally realized one day that they could not hold out much longer. His scouts brought back information that the dreaded Batlokoa, dispossessed by Chaka's legions, were approaching Butha-Buthe.

"Their leader is an old woman," the lieutenant reported, "a fierce old crone who, they say, is a witch. Their people are too numerous to count, and before them they drive the stumbling, crawling captives they have seized. Hundreds die every day for lack of food and water. And worse—I am sickened to tell you this, Morena [Sesotho for "Chief"]—many are so desperate that they eat each other!"

Moshoeshoe did not recoil in horror, because he had heard rumors of cannibalism. He questioned the scouting patrol carefully. The lieutenant concluded grimly: "They are like a horde of deadly locusts. They strip the country of everything and everyone. And they are moving slowly but surely toward Butha-Buthe."

Moshoeshoe prepared his defenses well, but his 2,000 people were greatly outnumbered by the 50,000 Batlokoa. As Moshoeshoe and his men retreated slowly, they realized that they could not stem this desperate human tide. Runners were sent back to Butha-Buthe to warn their people to flee to the caves in the mountains. Moshoeshoe and his warriors stood their ground to gain time for the others to escape.

Moshoeshoe had carefully chosen the site of battle, and he lost very few men. The slaughter of the Batlokoa was sickening. When at last he gave the order for withdrawal, his men carried out the bodies of their fallen comrades so that they would not be eaten by cannibals.

When the little warrior band joined the rest of the villagers in the caves, Moshoeshoe took stock. The women had carried out on their heads whatever food could be moved, but the crops had not yet been harvested and their year's supply of corn was left standing in the fields. The old men and the boys had managed to save part of the herds, but the situation was nevertheless extremely serious.

Next morning they were dismayed to see smoke rising from the direction of their village. A lookout came running breathlessly. "Butha-Buthe is in flames! The Batlokoa warriors are led by Sekonyela, the son of the cursed witch 'Manthatisi. They have destroyed our fields and burned our homes!"

A great clamor arose for revenge on the Batlokoa. Moshoeshoe outlined his plan before the hastily summoned council. "We cannot attack at Butha-Buthe. All the Batlokoa fighting men are now assembled there, and they are too many. We should circle behind the cliffs and attack the main camp to the east."

Moshoeshoe gathered his scattered warriors and led them down from the hills. His guess had been correct; the main camp was only lightly guarded. His patrols made short work of the sentries, so swiftly and silently that no alarm was sounded. Suddenly, with great shouts and blood-curdling shrieks, the main body of warriors fell upon the unsuspecting Batlokoa camp. There were only feeble old men, dispirited women and emaciated children. As Moshoeshoe's men swept through the skin tents and rudely constructed shelters, the dirt and the stench repelled them. A desperate sadness fell upon Moshoeshoe as he thought of the neat round huts of Butha-Buthe and the orderly green fields which had been wantonly destroyed by these savage nomads.

Suddenly an eerie, shrill cry riveted the attention of Moshoeshoe. Emerging from a tent was a wrinkled woman bent over with age. Her frizzled white hair hung in greasy tails around her bony shoulders. "Kill them! Kill them! Batlokoa, are you not the People of the Wildcat? Kill!"

As she came lunging toward him, claws bared, Moshoeshoe realized that this must be the terrible witch 'Manthatisi. Her people took courage from her unearthly shrieks, and the old men and women grabbed whatever was handy to face the soldiers. They ran at Moshoeshoe's men with clubs, sticks and rocks. They threw live embers from their fires. They even fought with their clay cooking pots. Of course, the weak and feeble Batlokoa were no match for Moshoeshoe, but they fought with cunning and savagery. Moshoeshoe's men killed many in revenge for the burning of Butha-Buthe. Every earthenware pot they could find they smashed in their rage. For a people constantly on the move like the Batlokoa, this was a serious loss. In Basotho history this famous fight is called the Battle of the Pots.

Sickened by the unending bloodshed and destruction and worried about his people's future, Moshoeshoe sent out patrols under the command of his uncle Leting to find a protected location where they could move to begin a new life. While he waited for their return, Moshoeshoe moved among the caves, trying to maintain his people's spirits and keeping a wary watch on the Batlokoa.

When Leting and his explorers returned, they had to slip through the Batlokoa horde, which now nearly surrounded Moshoeshoe. They had followed the Caledon River, they reported, until they had come to a smaller river which flowed into it. They had named this tributary the Phuthiatsana and had followed it upstream for a distance. "Just beyond the river there is a high mountain," Leting said, "with a flat top as if a giant hand had leveled it. Because the sides are so steep, a few men could defend the mountains against the mightiest army!"

"Is there water?"

"Yes, there are many springs, and there is much land around the mountain and in the valleys beyond for crops and for our cattle to graze. No one lives there, so we will not have to fight."

"Then it is settled," said Moshoeshoe. He was about to praise

Leting when one of the men on the patrol stepped forward. "One thing more. On the way back we found this man." They propelled their prisoner forward, a Zulu in full battle dress, his arms bound with strips of oxhide. This could mean only one thing! Moshoeshoe tried to conceal his alarm as he sent for one of the refugees who could act as interpreter.

The Zulu explained that he was a scout for an army of 15,000 Matabele warriors under the leadership of Moselikatze. They had deserted Chaka's army and were moving north in search of a new homeland. Within a few days, he thought, the main body of Moselikatze's forces would be in the vicinity—tough, well-armed and hungry.

Panic leaped through the crowd that had gathered around the prisoner. Amid the cries of anguish, Moshoeshoe tried to think his way out of the death trap. They were almost surrounded by 'Manthatisi's Batlokoa, more than twenty times as strong, eager to take revenge for the smashing of their pots. By the time his people could get ready to move, the Matabele would have come down out of the mountains like hungry lions ready to pounce on their prey. How could he break through the tightening ring, carrying along women, children, cattle and all the household goods of the village?

Moshoeshoe decided to test a principle which was to guide him till the end of his life: never fight if you can gain your ends by other means. He spoke to the Zulu prisoner: "A thousand apologies. My men did not know that we have no quarrel with Moselikatze or his Matabele people. Leting, unbind the man!" As the villagers looked on in disbelief, Moshoeshoe continued: "You must return to your army quickly and bring greetings to our friend Moselikatze. I grieve that I cannot go and deliver my good wishes in person, but I am preparing for a big raid at the new moon. There is much to be done, for the Batlokoa have many, many cattle, and I mean to take them all." He took the arm of the unbound prisoner and led him to a nearby observation post. "See, there are the Batlokoa, and there." Boastfully, Moshoeshoe described the terrain to the

Zulu, displaying his knowledge of the best attack routes and the location of the main body of the Batlokoa warriors. "And now," he said, "you must return to your people."

Thus primed, the Zulu prisoner could not fail to report his knowledge to his chief. Unable to resist such a prize, the Matabele fell on the Batlokoa horde. While his enemies fought one another, Moshoeshoe moved his entire village some sixty miles to the mountain with the flat top.

Hungry and exhausted, the Basotho nonetheless rejoiced mightily this night at the success of Moshoeshoe's strategem. The first rays of dawn signaled the start of their new life.

As Moshoeshoe moved among the people thatching their huts with sweet-smelling grasses, he looked for his grandfather, whom he had not seen since their arrival. It was his father, Mokhachane, who finally came toward Moshoeshoe and fell on his neck weeping. Word had just been received that, on the march to Thaba Bosiu, Peete had lagged behind to help two old women. All three old people had been seized by cannibals and eaten. The people's joy at arriving at a place of safety was overlaid with pain. 'Mamohato, grieving with Moshoeshoe, softly repeated an old proverb: "Break not your heart, my husband. Sorrow will roll away like the mists at sunrise."

The move to the mountain had indeed gained time for the Basotho, but Moshoeshoe knew that their enemies still roamed the countryside. He dissipated his grief for Peete by throwing himself into the job of making the mountain secure against any attack. After surveying the three steep gullies on the only side by which the mountain could be climbed, he sent out parties of men to dig and build barriers to make the ascent more difficult. Other warriors built stone walls to protect the defenders. Enormous piles of rocks were prepared at strategic points to be rolled down on attackers as they struggled to make the steep climb.

Although the defense work was going well, Moshoeshoe added a bit of extra insurance. He carefully planted rumors far and wide that there was black magic at work on the mountain. During the day anyone could see that it was only 300 feet high; but only a great fool would try to attack by night. For when it got dark, as everyone knew, the mountain grew to an immense height. This rumor was reinforced by the name that Moshoeshoe had given to the mountain—Thaba Bosiu, Mountain of the Night.

He also decided on another form of insurance to gain peace. The mad dictator Chaka, although far away, still posed a threat. Moshoeshoe knew he could not defend his people against the numerous and rigorously trained Zulus, so he paid tribute to Chaka. Young girls were sent across the mountains bearing otter and panther skins, ostrich feathers, the wings of cranes and other items much prized for the dress uniforms of Zulu warriors.

Many people came to the mountain and begged for shelter. Moshoeshoe took in anyone who asked for protection. At first there were only strays, torn from their tribes by some catastrophe, but later larger groups approached Thaba Bosiu. Moshoeshoe asked only that they put aside their hatred and work with others to build the new Basotho nation. To the ever-threatening cannibals, he sent seeds and hoes and advisers to help them plant their first crops. Some reformed cannibals even came to the mountain to live. Thaba Bosiu became well known as a haven from murder, treachery, slavery and constant fighting. Within some four years about 1,000 people had joined the original 2,000 Basotho. Despite their different backgrounds, Moshoeshoe was able to use his kindness, steady care and firm group discipline to weld these bits and pieces of humanity into a nation.

It was a happy time at Thaba Bosiu, a growing time, a building time. The babies who were born were cherished and given joyous names. It became unthinkable to name a child Lepoqo, the Trouble, as Moshoeshoe had started life.

And then, suddenly, disaster struck. A new wave of refugees came climbing breathlessly up the mountain to warn of the approach of Matoane, a Zulu chief who had broken with Chaka. Matoane was determined to carve out a large territory for his Amangoane tribe, and his treatment of conquered people was re-

ported to be as brutal as that of Chaka. Moshoeshoe called in the
inhabitants of the outlying villages and those who tilled the fields
around the mountain stronghold, and prepared for the defense of
Thaba Bosiu.

By nightfall the sentries on the stone walls could see the black-
and-white feather headbands of the Amangoane war party on the
other side of the Phuthiatsana River. The Basotho warriors looked
down with fear in their hearts as the enemy sharpened their short
spears. As the last rays of light retreated below the horizon, Matoane
began their war dance. The drums throbbed far into the night,
and drove the Basotho to strain every muscle pulling and pushing
huge rocks to the edge of the cliff.

Dawn was announced by the shrill cries of the Amangoane as
they charged up the mountain. The Basotho watched, motionless
and still as death. Encouraged by the lack of opposition, the Zulus
scaled the steep gullies, their triumphant shouts echoing as they
pressed upward. All at once, the Basotho began to roll rocks
down on them, the huge boulders splintering like shrapnel as they
hit the ledges below. Many of the attackers were crushed by the
flying rocks. Again the Amangoane tried to charge the heights,
and once more they were met by a rock shower. After several
more unsuccessful attempts, Matoane called for a retreat.

The Basotho burned to punish their enemy further, and before
he could think calmly, Moshoeshoe leaped down from behind the
stone walls followed by a large group of inflamed warriors. Hit from
the rear, the Amangoane stood their ground. The Basotho at
the summit could not roll down boulders for fear of hitting their
own men. Moshoeshoe realized that, in his enthusiasm, he had
made a serious mistake, for in close combat he and his men were
no match for the invaders. The fighting was savage and bloody.
Moshoeshoe was everywhere, striking with his spear, fending off
blows with his great swallow-tailed shield, shouting for his men
to pull back to the fortifications. Suddenly he found himself isolated
part of the way down the slope with only two of his men beside
him. The Zulus surrounding him drew back and gave their signal

of victory, striking their shields in cadence and electrifying the air with their hissing war cries. All at once a strange silence fell over the slope. Moshoeshoe saw that the end had come. If he continued to fight, he would be overrun and stabbed by a thousand spears. Surrender meant death of another kind. There flashed through his mind with a searing pain the vision of all his unfulfilled dreams.

Moshoeshoe drew himself up to his full height, lowered his shield and spear and ordered his men: "Come, follow me; it is not thus that kings are slain!" The Zulus stood transfixed. He called out proudly, "Turn aside, O Amazulu, make room!" and walked unwaveringly up the hill. The amazed warriors, as if hypnotized, fell back to let him pass. When he reached the height, he slowly turned and looked down at the battle field. Then he and his men, who had followed in frightened silence, leaped behind the stone wall to safety.

Disgusted by the lost opportunity and wary of another boulder attack, Matoane withdrew. But Moshoeshoe knew that he would try again and that the people on the Mountain of the Night would never be secure until the power of Matoane was broken.

Again, Moshoeshoe used his head instead of his spear. He suddenly stopped paying tribute to the dreaded Chaka. After a time, just as Moshoeshoe expected, a party of fierce Zulu warriors came calling on the Basotho chief. "You are welcome to Thaba Bosiu. I would have you bring back to Chaka word of my admiration and the honor I heap upon his name. Great is my desire to continue to send gifts to him," Moshoeshoe explained calmly and courteously, "but whatever I send must first go through the land of the Amangoane and their chief, the evil Matoane, captures these treasures meant for the great Chaka and keeps them for himself."

Chaka, already infuriated over Matoane's defection, needed only this news to take reprisals. The Amagoane were badly beaten, and some eventually found their way back to Thaba Bosiu, where they petitioned Moshoeshoe for refuge. "He was always kind," one of these defeated Amangoane later wrote in a tribal history, "and he was always in favor of quiet, peaceful things."

Several years later, Matoane himself came once more to Thaba Bosiu, but he laid his arms on the ground at the bottom of the cliff. He came to Basutoland a fugitive after a severe defeat by the British near the Umtata River, but his spirit was not yet broken. Moshoeshoe listened quietly as Matoane outlined a plan to lead his handful of remaining warriors on a conquest of Zululand.

"We have been enemies in the past," Moshoeshoe pleaded with him, "but if you were my kinsman I would give you this advice. You will be crushed like an ant by the Zulus. Do not go, Matoane. We will give your people food and help. You are still a great chief. Stay here with us and help us build Basutoland."

Matoane could not be dissuaded, but he asked Moshoeshoe to take his young son Izikale and bring him up among the Basotho. Many months later word reached Thaba Bosiu that Matoane had been killed and the remaining Amangoane scattered or enslaved. Moshoeshoe carried out his pledge to rear the orphaned son of Matoane, and when Izikale was old enough, Moshoeshoe put him in charge of one of his villages, as befits the son of a chief.

It was about this time that a great change came over life in Basutoland with the introduction of horses. Griquas and Korannas— half-breeds familiar with the white man's ways—began to drift up from the south and west, raiding villages as they went. They had an unbeatable advantage over the villagers because they had horses and firearms, both of which were unknown to their victims. Since their muskets had a longer range than any throwing spear, none of the Basotho had ever got close to the horsemen. No one was sure whether the man and the animal could be separated, or whether the two together were some new kind of creature.

One day a small Griqua raiding party captured an outlying village, shot its inhabitants and drove off its cattle. This was the usual procedure, but then the unusual happened. Finding a cask of home-brewed beer, the Griquas proceeded to get roaring drunk. Baphuthi warriors, allies of Moshoeshoe who had come running to the aid of the villagers, easily captured the raiders and for the first time had definite proof that man and horse were two separate beings. However, there still remained a problem. From which half did the explosions come? The tribesmen knew nothing about guns. Deciding to play it safe, they watched the horses for many hours, and were much relieved when no flashes of "lightning" were forthcoming.

The Baphuthi chief, Morosi, gave one of these horses to Moshoeshoe as a gift. Moshoeshoe consulted his wise men on how to ride, but since no one in Thaba Bosiu had ever seen a horse, their advice was useless. Neither Morosi nor Moshoeshoe was even sure in which direction to mount. The Basotho stared in disbelief as their great chief learned to ride by trial and error.

Moshoeshoe laughed as hard as any, but he quickly realized the great advantage that a mounted warrior had over one who fought on foot. He used everything the Basotho had to buy horses and guns, and over the years transformed his people into a nation of horsemen. At one time Moshoeshoe had a law passed by the National Council ordering every man to own a horse. Horse racing became a national passion. Although today there are automobiles and trucks in Basutoland—or, as it is now called, Lesotho—this is the only country in the world where, with very little doubling up, the entire male population of the country could saddle up and ride off at once.

Early in the 1830s, Moshoeshoe saw his first white man when a trader stopped at Thaba Bosiu to find native guides. With the help of one of his warriors who had fled to Cape Town during the Wars of Calamity and who had now returned to his people, Moshoeshoe plied the visitor with eager questions. "The city and surrounding countryside are being torn apart by rival white 'tribes,'" the trader explained. "The Boers and the English are at each other's throats. If the English free the black slaves of the Boers, they will surely leave Cape Town to search for new places to settle." When he left, the trader presented Moshoeshoe with a pistol and some horses.

Later that year, just as the trader had predicted, small parties of

Boers appeared along the Caledon—first, hunters, then cattle drovers in search of pasture. A short while later permanent settlers arrived, and Moshoeshoe rode down with an escort of sixteen men to welcome them to his land and offer his assistance.

As more whites came, it was inevitable that there would be misunderstandings. Accustomed to seeing black men as slaves, the Boers' manner often offended the proud Basotho, and the natives retaliated. Lawless men, both black and white, added to the prickly situation by stealing cattle, and Moshoeshoe became concerned about the future. He confided his fears to a visiting hunter, a half-caste Christian named Adam Krotz, who lived in Philippolis on the Orange River. Krotz told Moshoeshoe that his people had for many years led a peaceful life. "Have you many guns?" asked Moshoeshoe. "No," said Krotz, "but we have a missionary. That is what you need here at Thaba Bosiu—a missionary, not more guns."

The Basotho listened intently as Krotz explained how the missionaries had helped his Griquas and other tribes. Convinced, Moshoeshoe begged him to make suitable arrangements when he got back to Philippolis. To help Krotz, Moshoeshoe sent one hundred head of cattle with him. These were looted by Korannas along the way, and Moshoeshoe sent more. Again they did not reach their destination, but Moshoeshoe sent at least two more herds of cattle to Krotz. All Philippolis knew about Moshoeshoe's earnest quest for a missionary.

Meanwhile, three young Frenchmen—Eugene Casalis, Thomas Arbousset and Constant Gosselin—landed at Cape Town on their way to join a Protestant mission inland. They were met with the news that their station had been attacked and was no longer operating. It was a tremendous disappointment for these dedicated servants of God, who were eager to begin their work with the Africans. Instead, they were sent to Kuruman to get acquainted with the country and await instructions from France. On the way they stopped at Philippolis and heard Adam Krotz's story. Here was a clear call to do God's work! They asked Krotz to ready wagons and supplies and go along as their guide. Then they sent off a message to the Paris Evangelical Society and in June of 1833 left for Basutoland without awaiting a reply.

During the course of the journey, Krotz tried to size up the missionaries he was guiding. Casalis, the leader, was just twenty-one years old, slim and boyish, with a dark complexion and dark, curly hair. Arbousset had a clean-shaven chin and a heavy fringe of beard on either cheek. Krotz saw that both were well-educated, cultivated and gracious men. He was also impressed with Gosselin, who seemed able to build or fix anything with his strong, capable hands.

The wagons jogged along what seemed to be vast plains, but Casalis soon realized that they were really a series of plateaus rising like giant steps toward the blue hills in the distance. They were excited by the unfamiliar wildlife—the multitudes of spring-boks, blessboks, gnus, caamas, elands, reeboks, rietboks, wild asses striped like zebras (which, Krotz told them, were called quaggas), and an occasional lion, panther or pack of hyenas.

One evening, just outside their camp, Casalis came across a pile of bones bleached white by the sun. Poking into the grim pile, he was shocked to find several skulls.

"They are not remains of baboons," Krotz glumly confirmed his suspicions, "they are human skulls." He told them of the terror and destruction of the Wars of Calamity. In the days to come the Frenchmen found everywhere terrible indications of the catastrophe —more bones, broken earthenware, fallen walls overgrown with brambles, abandoned villages crumbling in the dust, easily recognized boundaries of fields reverting to wilderness. The grim realities of the plains of Africa began to settle on the three Frenchmen— the harsh open sky and the vast, lonely distances. They were relieved when they entered the hills and finally made camp at Thaba Ntso, an elevation of great height with a circumference of several miles. All around Thaba Ntso were majestic mountains separated by wide valleys. In the distance lay fields of maize and sorgho, almost ripe.

The morning after they crossed the Caledon River, the party

reluctantly broke camp, leaving the banks shaded with willows, their roots plunged into the life-giving water and their graceful branches alive with scarlet chaffinches and ringdoves. As the wagons began to roll, flocks of teal and wild duck rose in flight. Suddenly, two horses came wildly racing toward them. They careened to a precipitous halt, and two young men who had been riding bareback, clinging to the manes, jumped off, gesturing excitedly and talking at a furious pace. Krotz rushed up to interpret, and Casalis, Arbousset and Gosselin stared at the horsemen in amazement. Their bronze-colored skins, not black as the missionaries had expected, shone with perspiration. Rich panther capes adorned their shoulders, and their heads were covered by outrageously shaped straw hats with serrated edges, looped at the top and spiked and indented around the crown. Otherwise they were naked.

"These are Letsie and Molapo," Krotz explained to the astonished missionaries. "They are sons of Moshoeshoe who have come to welcome you to Basutoland."

Before Casalis could ask any questions, the young men jumped back on their horses, kicked them vigorously and went recklessly hurtling off, laughing and waving, their capes flying.

"But they are entire novices in the art of riding!" chuckled Arbousset.

"The Basotho have only just learned about horses," Krotz explained. "They have tried to show you a special honor by sending their welcoming party on horseback."

As the two wagons, creaking under the weight of supplies, came up the valley through Rafutho Pass, Casalis wrote in his diary: "We became Basothos from today onwards. Our destinies and those of the tribe are identical."

Moshoeshoe had called a solemn council to greet the newcomers. In his journal Casalis noted that the chief was over six feet tall. His face was almost Roman in appearance, with a slightly flattened straight nose. He was light of color like the rest of his clan. Casalis judged him to be about forty-five years old at the time. The upper part of his body was naked, and the missionary noticed that there was no trace of the fat so common in the self-indulgent African chieftains of the time.

Casalis later wrote in his diary: "The chief bent on me a look at once majestic and benevolent. . . . His eyes, a little weary but full of intelligence and softness, made a deep impression on me. I felt at once that I had to do with a superior man, trained to think, to command others and above all, to control himself."

As Casalis outlined the many good things they hoped to do if they were allowed to establish their mission in Basutoland, Moshoeshoe carefully scrutinized these three white men who were going to bring a new life to his people. Everyone listened courteously until Krotz had finished the translations. He then presented Moshoeshoe with some gifts the missionaries had brought—a splendid military uniform trimmed with dark green lace and a pointed hat to match, a fine hunting gun with a carved design on the stock, a powder horn and bullet pouch decorated with silver and a walking stick with a silver top. Finally Moshoeshoe spoke, slowly but very loudly so that all assembled could hear.

"My heart is white with joy," he said. "Your words are great and good. It is enough for me to see your clothing, your arms and rolling houses in which you travel, to understand how much intelligence and strength you have. You see our desolation. This country was full of inhabitants. Wars have devastated it. Multitudes have perished; others are refugees in foreign lands. I remain almost alone on this rock. Even now our enemies infest the countryside. For many moons my people are without salt, for we dare not send a party to the salt springs three days' journey to the north.

"I have been told that you can help us. You promise to do it. That is enough. It is all I want to know. Remain with us. You shall instruct us. We will do all you wish. The country is at your disposal. We can go through it together, and you shall choose the place which will best suit you."

With that Moshoeshoe rose and began a tour of Thaba Bosiu. First they stopped at the hut of 'Mamohato. Then Moshoeshoe guided them through narrow lanes between low huts and back out again into the vast space where the cattle were penned during the night. This was divided into many separate enclosures by stone walls. From there they went to the southwest corner of the mountaintop where Mokhachane had his hut. On succeeding days they toured the countryside surrounding Thaba Bosiu, and finally decided to locate the mission at Morija, twenty-five miles to the southwest. Letsie was in charge of the outpost there. Moshoeshoe had sent his eldest son there in order to encourage some of his subjects gradually to descend from the heights where they had fled during the wars. There was good soil and an abundant water supply, and the missionaries could plant the slips of peach, apricot and fig trees they had brought from France, as well as the seeds of many new and useful crops.

During the next few months the missionaries concentrated on learning the Sesotho language. Moshoeshoe himself undertook to teach them, and he delighted in the results. In a short time they were able to hold serious conversations, and Casalis and Arbousset explained that they were trying to put the words into written form for the first time. They experimented with their form of written Sesotho by taking on as pupils some of the brightest young boys. One day Moshoeshoe was trying to explain the importance of reading to his father Mokhachane. "Lies! Lies!" shouted the old man stubbornly. "I will never believe that words can become visible."

Moshoeshoe told him, "Think of something and tell it to Casalis. He will draw some marks and you will see." The missionary listened to Mokhachane and patiently wrote in the sand. Then Moshoeshoe sent for one of the village scholars. The boy looked down at the sand read back Mokhachane's thoughts. The old man was stupefied, and never again questioned the white man's "magic."

Moshoeshoe also took a personal interest in furthering Christianity among his people. Although never formally converted himself, he set a good example by attending services regularly. On Sundays he would often call his people to church by shouting from the top of the mountain, "To prayer! To prayer! Everybody, everybody, children and women as well!"

For those who were cautious about giving up the old ways, Moshoeshoe had this advice: "Look at an egg. If a man breaks it, there comes out only a watery and yellow substance, but if it be placed under the wing of a fowl there comes a living thing from it. Who can understand this? Who knows how the heat of the hen brings out the chicken? This is beyond our understanding, yet we know that it is true. Let us do as the hen does. Let us put these truths in our hearts as the hen puts the eggs under her wings. Let us take the same pains, and something new will come out of them."

However, the chief was wisely not putting all his eggs in one basket. After the French Protestants were well established, Moshoeshoe invited a number of other missionaries to settle in Basutoland and contributed generously toward their work. Several other Protestant denominations and Roman Catholics set up churches, schools and other good works in different parts of the country.

"Missionaries are like doctors," Moshoeshoe once said. "One should not always consult the same one." As a result of this policy, the Basotho have always been remarkably tolerant of beliefs different from their own.

The missionaries did not press Moshoeshoe to convert to Christianity, but he felt that he owed Casalis an explanation. First, he reviewed the compelling political reasons for his attachment to animism—the ruling power of the tribe was tied up with the old religious customs and ancestral homage. Also, he said, he was a polygamist, and even for God he could not abandon his wives or put aside his children. Casalis well understood the old custom of consolidating tribal relationships through marriage—was it not the same with European royalty? And he had ample evidence that Moshoeshoe was genuinely devoted to his many wives and children.

Moshoeshoe welcomed the first white men, but as more came, he began to have fears concerning the good intentions of the Boers, or Afrik'aners, as they were also called. In the year 1836 thousands

of them decided to leave Cape Town, where British law forbade
them to keep slaves. In covered wagons much like those used by
westward-moving pioneers in America, the Boers began their great
trek inland. At first Moshoeshoe was not directly concerned, but
he noted that other chiefs who had concluded mutual friendship
treaties with the Boers were not guaranteed against mistreatment.
It mystified and horrified Moshoeshoe that white men who professed
to be Christians did not always respect the dignity of a chief or
the life of a chief's messenger, and from that time on he tried to
avoid meetings with white men or, if forced to go, always made
sure to take along one of his missionaries.

Nothing much stood in the way of Boer expansion after the
1838 defeat of the Zulus at Blood River. Although they still considered the Boers their subjects, the British did not wish to saddle
themselves with the problems of annexing the native territory into
which the white men were moving. As for Moshoeshoe, he welcomed the Boers, but considered them "subject to the laws of . . .
[the] Chief and [they] must expect to incur the penalty of any
acts of cruelty or murder they may commit . . . during their
residence in his territory." The Boers, of course, had no intention
of acknowledging a black chief as their ruler.

Land claims also became a source of trouble. After a series of
bloody clashes, Moshoeshoe asked Arbousset to meet with the
Boers in his behalf.

"You can't trust those sneaky Kaffirs for a moment," the white
men complained. "They sell us the land, and then they come
skulking around looking to steal cattle and murder us in our beds."

"There had been some misunderstanding here," Arbousset explained. "You have no permanent claim that makes this land your
private property. In Africa all land is held in trust for the entire
tribe. No one can give it away or sell it."

"Well, just you look here!" And the documents with Moshoeshoe's
mark were hauled out.

"These are of no value," Arbousset said. "Moshoeshoe did not
understand what he was signing or else was tricked into this.

According to tribal custom, the one who plows the land has the right to it only until the harvest is gathered. Moshoeshoe gave you the right to use the land, to plow and harvest it, but actual ownership always stays with the tribe. You must understand that their ways and their laws are different."

"And they must understand that this land is now ours, and any blacks who come within rifle range are asking for trouble!"

In this way, misunderstandings and lawlessness on both sides kept the border country in turmoil for many years. Many small battles were fought, but neither Basotho nor Boer was strong enough to decisively defeat the other.

Finally, in 1843, the British decided to move troops into the disputed region and define the boundaries between blacks and whites. The Boers resented that the British had reserved for the Basotho much of the land they coveted; Moshoeshoe was troubled by the new arrangement because he realized that the Basotho had been left with too little land to support their growing nation.

After a series of conferences with British officials, Moshoeshoe called a Pitso, or National Basotho Council, to discuss the situation. Moshoeshoe analyzed the problem calmly. "We must work with the British," he counseled. "The time is soon coming when we will not be able to withstand the Boers. There is no security for the Basotho nation unless the British take the responsibility of protecting us."

There was a murmur of agreement. "We have been greatly honored," Moshoeshoe continued. "Queen Victoria, who sits on her throne in England, has asked the Basotho to become her allies. Her representative has offered our people a sum of money to help her Major Warden keep the peace. It is not a great amount— £ 75—but we should take it and become soldiers of the Queen."

"Never! We should throw the money back into the face of the Queen's governor. We should sharpen our spears and drive the Boers and the British and every other white man from our land."

"You speak with a tongue possessed by spirits! The white men have guns. Of what avail are all our spears against their lightning?"

"Let us take the Queen's money and buy guns!"

Because there was no written language by which they could communicate with each other, the Basotho had always been great talkers, and the discussion continued all day and all night. When it seemed that all the arguments were becoming stale and repetitive, an older man inquired of Moshoeshoe in a voice full of reproach: "You have always said, Morena, that you are a man of peace. You speak often of your kinsman Mohlomi. Why are you desperate for guns? Why do you tell us to become soldiers and kill for a woman chief no Basotho has ever seen?"

Moshoeshoe rose to answer, and a silence fell during which the only sounds were the whisper of breezes frolicking in the poplars and the crackle of flames leaping to escape the smoky peat fires. "The teachings of Mohlomi lie in my heart like the first flower of spring. If I never liked war in my youth, how can I like it now that I am old? But the Basotho people also lie cradled in my heart. There are some here who walked by my side when we went from our Bamonageng villages to Butha-Buthe. Who among you can forget the caves to which we fled like wounded, frightened gazelles, those caves full of skulls and bones and dark places where the blood had soaked deep into the rock? We are no longer only Bamonageng; we have been joined by brothers from many different tribes. We have flung back those evil warriors, hungry to devour us, from our stronghold on the Mountain of the Night. We have made a Basotho nation!

"Now the Boers come preaching 'peace on earth,' but they do not hesitate to fire their guns. The only sin we have ever committed against them is to possess a good and fertile country. Should we bow our heads meekly and become their slaves? The British try to keep the Boers in place, but they have too few soldiers in this vast land. Whoever is strongest will make the laws. Spears, *assegais*, knobsticks—these do not talk very loudly. But guns—ah, they are very loud, and the Boers will hear this great noise.

"Let us take the Queen's money and buy guns. Let us become soldiers of the Queen. Then, if the Boers attack, the English must help us protect ourselves. The Queen must take us under her blanket."

And so it was decided. By using the English money, by working for pay, by trickery, raiding or any other means, the Basotho were encouraged to acquire guns and horses. Contact was made with smugglers, unscrupulous bands of white men and women who hauled firearms and ammunition over the snow-laden passes of the Drakensburg. In addition to guns, Moshoeshoe purchased at enormous cost a cannon which had once fired salutes from the prow of a man-of-war. As a result of this feverish activity, Moshoeshoe could, within a few years, field a formidable force of 7,000 well-armed Basotho cavalry. Although many worked and paid for their own weapons, all the equipment, like the land, was considered communal property.

Moshoeshoe even employed several armorers under the supervision of John Wilks, a former master gunner with the British Royal Artillery. One of his first projects was to help the Basuto build a cannon, twenty feet long and six inches across the muzzle, from brass bangles donated by the wives of Moshoeshoe.

Major Henry Douglas Warden, the British commander, often called on the Basotho chief for aid against the Boers or against other tribes. Moshoeshoe, anxious to hoard Basotho strength, used any means possible to avoid fighting. Only when the argument touched the Basotho directly would Moshoeshoe move willingly, and then always on ground of his own choosing. Also, the British major did not pay his African troops; he rewarded them by allowing them to plunder their victims. For Moshoeshoe and his Basotho this was a repugnant policy. Was this not just the kind of cruelty and bloodshed they had pledged to abolish by moving to Thaba Bosiu? Warden complained about the situation in a personal report to the new British governor of the Cape Province, Sir George Cathcart.

"How can you put your faith, sir, in the word of a black man who signs treaties he has no intention of honoring, who promises things he knows he will never deliver? Moshoeshoe is the most crooked chief in Africa."

Sir George raised his bushy eyebrows and flicked the ashes from his cigar. "Your trouble, Warden, is that you have never taken the pains to understand Moshoeshoe. His first concern is to secure his little nation against attacks by both whites and blacks. You know that in the north we are rulers in name only—the law is in the hands of the strongest. And surely you understand our deliberate policy of not letting any of the tribes become too strong. Until we are ready to go in and take over, we will continue to play off one tribe against another, and the Boers against all the blacks. These are crooked times, Warden. Broken pledges are not Moshoeshoe's alone."

"May I observe, sir, that it is all very well to try to understand what motivates Moshoeshoe," Warden said with soldierly gruffness, "but what do you intend to do about the never-ending cattle raids?"

"Well, we cannot let them get away with that! We have to satisfy the Boers' claims against the Basotho, and we can also take the opportunity to give a boost to some of the other tribes. Here is an order I have prepared."

Warden was surprised at the stiff fine imposed on the Basotho. They were ordered to deliver to the Boers 10,000 cattle and 1,000 horses. Moshoeshoe was directed to make peace with his ancient enemy Sekonyela of the Batlokoa and to restore all the cattle stolen from him. In addition, a desirable tract of Moshoeshoe's land was given to a tribe of Hottentots that had settled near Thabanchu under the tutelage of Wesleyan missionaries.

"I am sending Captain W. S. Hogg and Mr. C. M. Owen to collect the reparations," Cathcart concluded. "I shall await their report on the situation."

Cathcart had a long time to wait. By various means, Moshoeshoe delayed payment of the fine for as long as he could. At last the governor received a communication from Hogg and Owen.

"We have received a token payment on the reparations," they

wrote. "Moshoeshoe sent his son Nehemiah with about 3,500 head of cattle, but they are sorry specimens, drawn from the worst of his herds. He sent 500 mounted men to accompany the payment—a guard of honor, he said; a show of force, we think. . . . We were impressed with their discipline and their air of quiet determination, and we feel that they will give a good account of themselves if called upon to fight."

In time another dispatch arrived from Hogg and Owen: "We still wait for the remainder of the reparations payment, but it is our opinion that Moshoeshoe will send nothing more, except under duress."

At this, Cathcart decided to take personal charge. He arrived at the Platberg Mission on December 13, 1852, and sent for Moshoeshoe. Instead, Nehemiah and another of Moshoeshoe's sons, Masupha, came. Sir George was most insistent that Moshoeshoe attend in person the following day and made it clear that he expected the rest of the fine to be paid in three days' time.

An emergency session of the Pitso was called. The Basotho opposed Moshoeshoe's leaving Thaba Bosiu. They remembered past murder, indignities and humiliations of native chiefs by white men. Moshoeshoe was willing to risk the meeting. He was curious to meet the new governor, who, despite his firmness, had a reputation for being sympathetic to the natives. The Reverend Casalis and his brother-in-law, Moore Dyke, a newer addition to the missionary staff, agreed to accompany Moshoeshoe.

As they saddled up the next morning, hundreds of Basotho mounted their horses and rode along with the intention of defending the small party.

"Go back, go back!" Moshoeshoe urged. But they said nothing and continued. "How will it look to the English governor that a great chief must bring along protectors?" No one changed his course.

Continued pleading availed nothing, and finally, in exasperation, Moshoeshoe flailed about him with his riding whip. He was touched by this display of love, but he felt that it would serve his purpose better to meet Cathcart alone. When they saw his determination the leaders drew back. "We will be nearby. Signal if help is needed."

Cathcart came out to greet the old Basotho chieftain. When they had settled comfortably indoors, Cathcart proceeded to business. "I told you in that letter that I hope to meet you in peace, and I still hope so, as I look to you as the great Chief in this part."

"I hope so, too," Moshoeshoe said with fervor, "for peace is like the rain which makes the grass grow, while war is like the wind which dries it up. You are right in looking to me; that is in accordance with the treaties."

The time had come for firmness, Cathcart decided. "I will not talk much, but wish to know whether you received my message yesterday, in which I made the demand of cattle and horses. I have nothing to alter in my letter."

"I received the letter, but do not know where I will get the cattle," the chief said quietly. "Am I to understand that 10,000 head demanded are a fine imposed for the thefts committed by my people, in addition to returning the cattle stolen?"

"I demand but 10,000 head," Cathcart replied, "though your people have stolen many more, and I consider this a just award which must be paid in three days."

Casalis sought to clarify the issue: "Do the three days count from yesterday or today?"

"Today is the first of the three," the governor said firmly.

"The time is short and the cattle are many," Moshoeshoe objected. "Will you not allow me six days to collect them?"

"You had time given you when Major Hogg and Mr. Owen made the first demand," Cathcart pointed out, "and then promised to comply with it, but you did not."

"But I was not quite idle," Moshoeshoe protested. "Do not the papers in the Commissioner's hands show I collected them?"

"They do, but not half the number demanded."

"That is true, but I have not now control enough over my people to induce them to comply with the demand, however anxious I may be to do so."

"If you are not able to collect them," Cathcart warned, "I must go and do it; and if any resistance be made, it will then be war, but I shall not be satisfied with 10,000 head then, but shall take all I can."

"Do not talk of war," Moshoeshoe begged, "for however anxious I may be to avoid it, you know that a dog when beaten will show his teeth."

"It will therefore be better that you should give up the cattle than that I should go for them," Cathcart replied smoothly.

"I wish for peace," Moshoeshoe sighed, "but I have the same difficulty with my people that you have in the Cape Colony. Your prisons are never empty, and I have thieves among my own people."

"Then I would recommend you to catch the thieves and bring them to me, and I will hang them."

"I do not wish to hang them, but to talk to them and give them advice. If you hang them, they cannot talk."

"If I hang them, they cannot steal, and I am not going to talk anymore," Cathcart said in exasperation. "I have said that if you do not give up the cattle in three days I must come and take them."

"Do not talk of coming to Thaba Bosiu," Moshoeshoe warned. "But I will go at once and do my best, and perhaps God will help me."

Casalis and Dyke understood that the Basotho could not possibly gather enough cattle and horses to pay the indemnity in the short time allotted. They sent M. Maitin, one of the new missionaries, along with Moshoeshoe's brother Mopeli to beg for an extension of time. Cathcart remained unmoved. He brought up his troops, crossed the Phuthiatsana River, and prepared emplacements for the twenty-five pairs of guns and two howitzers he had brought. One hundred fifty transport wagons hauled supplies to the foot of the mountain. Although Moshoeshoe had a numerical advantage with 7,000 fighting men, the British had modern rifles with a longer firing range than the antiquated flintlock muskets of the Basotho.

Cathcart broke his troops into three columns, each of which was to climb the mountain by a separate route. When they reached the top, they would, according to the plan, come together and round up all the cattle and horses.

One column found the terrain too difficult, and when the heavens suddenly loosed a furious thunderstorm the British spent the night on the rocks and in the morning returned to the base camp.

Another group was faced by 5,000 men led by Moshoeshoe, his eldest son Letsie and his friend and ally, Moletsane, Chief of the Bataung. The Basotho kept withdrawing just beyond firing range. The downpour forced the British to take cover. When the clouds rolled away, they found themselves surrounded and withdrew quickly with few losses on either side.

The third column got the farthest. They actually rounded up a great herd of cattle but, flushed with success, they ran into an ambush led by Molapo, Moshoeshoe's second son.

As the British rushed helter-skelter down the mountain, driving cattle and horses before them at breakneck speed, they met the group which had been driven off by Moshoeshoe. The commanders conferred briefly, and it was decided to stop on level ground and pen the cattle. The retreat became more orderly, and by dusk soldiers, equipment, cattle and horses were settled down. All at once from out of the night came weird, high-pitched singing. The cattle became restless, and as the singing and calling back and forth in Sesotho increased in volume, some oxen broke loose. The British later learned that these were special cattle, trained by the Basotho to race free, obedient to calls and songs from the sidelines. As soon as the trained oxen began to run, Moshoeshoe's warriors fired wildly, causing about 400 animals to stampede back toward the Basotho lines. By the time the British had restored some order among the rest of the frantic animals, the Basotho had withdrawn beyond their range of fire.

It was late when Moshoeshoe finished hearing reports from his

various commanders. Then he dictated, with the help of the
Reverend Casalis and Nehemiah, what has been called "the most
politic document ever penned in South Africa." It was addressed
to Governor Cathcart:

Thaba Bosiu
Midnight, December 20, 1852

Your Excellency,
This day you have fought against my people and taken much
cattle. As the object for which you have come is to have a
compensation for the Boers, I beg you will be satisfied with
what you have taken. I entreat peace from you. You have
shown your power, you have chastised; let it be enough, I pray
you, and let me be no longer considered an enemy to the Queen.
I will try all I can to keep my people in order for the future.

Your humble servant,
Moshoeshoe

Although the Basotho had been triumphant, Moshoeshoe felt
that it was indeed their cattle raiding which had precipitated
the Battle of Berea. There were twenty dead Basotho warriors and
twenty wounded as a result. In the morning the fully armed
Basotho army lined the ridge to see what the British would do.
During the night Cathcart had received reinforcements and additional ammunition from Platberg; but he had also received
Moshoeshoe's touching letter, and he was anxious for peace. As
the British retreated, carrying their thirty-eight dead and fourteen
wounded soldiers, Moshoeshoe would not allow his men to boast of
their victory. Even today in songs praising Basotho chiefs and
great deeds in war, the Battle of Berea is hardly mentioned. Instead, they remember an old proverb, the truth of which Moshoeshoe proved: "He who asks for peace at the right time builds up
his village."

Unfortunately, the Battle of Berea settled nothing. The boundary

line drawn by the British between Boer and Basotho was still un-
acceptable to either side, and the British still had too few troops
to enforce the decision. Rather than get caught up in a war, the
British decided to wash their hands of the whole matter by
abandoning the government to the Boers who had settled there.
As a result, a new country, the Orange Free State, was born in
1854, and the stage was set for the next act of the black-white
tragedy.

At first there was no conflict. The new President of the Orange
Free State, Josiah Hoffman, arranged a meeting with Moshoeshoe.
Although he was a cripple, Hoffman had himself carried up to
Thaba Bosiu. Among the gifts he showered on Moshoeshoe was a
fifty-pound cask of gunpowder. When this news broke back home
in Bloemfontein, the Volkraad (or legislature) was furious and
finally threw Hoffman out of office.

Hotheads among the Boers did not want peace. They wanted
the rich Basotho lands along the Caledon River, and asked that
stiff punishment be imposed on all Basotho for the actions of the
black cattle and horse thieves, who continued unchecked. The new
President, Jacobus Boshoff, was prepared to be tougher than his
predecessor.

To avert the impending war, Sir George Grey, the kindly,
tactful new British Governor of Cape Colony, offered to talk to
Moshoeshoe. "A man who raises barbarians in the scale of civilization is admired by sages," he told the aging chieftain. "You are
now the builder. You have collected some barbarians and made a
kind of nation. The question is now whether you are to succeed or
fail. Not only is South Africa looking on, but many other parts
of the world too. Every good man is willing to help, and no one
more than Mr. Boshoff, President of the Orange Free State. It is
impossible that a civilized nation can allow a nation of thieves
to remain on their boundary."

Moshoeshoe answered sorrowfully: "I cannot bind myself to say
there will be no more stealing; thieves do not tell me when they

come in or out of Basutoland. You must give me more time."
But Moshoeshoe knew that his control was slipping, and his wishes
were often ignored.

President Boshoff, egged on by Boer "war hawks," lost patience
and called for armed volunteers to put down the natives. As the
white men marched into Basutoland, Moshoeshoe wrote to the
Boer leader:

> Your messenger came in last night with a letter from you in
> which you have begun to speak of "Peace." I am sorry that you
> ever spoke of War. It is not Moshoeshoe who began War; and
> . . . I strongly enjoined on my people, without excepting the
> smallest Captains, not to disturb you on your march. . . . Before
> I began to strike, I wanted to ascertain what was the true
> intention and power of the Boers. . . . My policy in this war
> was to see first and consider. The Boers have been unanimous in
> saying that the present War was to last till one of the two
> nations was rooted out of the face of the earth. . . . Could the
> English ever blame me, who am yet a barbarian and a heathen,
> for following the example of a civilized and Christian nation?
> . . . However, my name is Moshoeshoe, and my sister is called
> "Peace."

Notwithstanding, the Boers continued the invasion, marching to
Thaba Bosiu. Although Moshoeshoe was still greatly respected,
many of the younger Africans questioned his peace policy. They
were convinced that a better policy would have been to strike
first and consider later. Finally, several battles were fought, but
with indecisive results. This pleased the British, who were playing
a double game, hoping to come back as rulers of the territory
some day when they could muster enough strength. Therefore,
they felt it was best if neither side was allowed to get too strong.
Sir George Grey again offered to negotiate for a peace.

The settlement he proposed in 1858 was known as the Treaty of
Aliwal. When Moshoeshoe heard its provisions, he knew disaster
awaited the Basotho. The Boers took much of their remaining

territory and were awarded a huge indemnity of 40,000 cattle, 5,000 horses and 60,000 sheep. In addition, two of Moshoeshoe's sons were taken as hostages, and the French missionaries were expelled for political activity on behalf of the Basotho.

Tears filled the old man's eyes as he embraced the missionaries for the last time. "You have been my eye, my hand, my foot," he said to Casalis. Casalis himself had spent most of his time at Thaba Bosiu as an unofficial minister of state. How Moshoeshoe would miss his intelligence, tact, knowledge of the world and ability to take Moshoeshoe's ideas and put them into words that were respected in Cape Town and the capitals of Europe! To the other missionaries he was also profoundly grateful for their formulation of a written Sesotho language and for preserving Basotho literature, traditions and history. He thanked them for all they had done for his people—for educating the young, instructing the adults in the use of new tools and crops and modern farming practices, founding hospitals and clinics; explaining white men's ideas and behavior and helping to solve their many problems.

Some of the missionaries wept openly. The results of this old man's gallant courage would live beyond the Boer oppression, Arbousset vowed. All Europe would know of Moshoeshoe's kindly wisdom, his simple humanity, his genius in administering his people's affairs. To forcibly part people who held each other in such mutual respect and affection was a crime against humanity!

From this time on Moshoeshoe became less successful in restraining his subchiefs. They feared that in this situation where "might makes right," his policy of turning the other cheek would result in extermination by the Boers. Moshoeshoe, on the other hand, was convinced that if they fought back they would indeed be exterminated. He flung all his energies into the only solution which he thought could save Basutoland—annexation by the British.

The matter dragged on for several years while relations with the Boers slid steadily downhill. In 1863, a new President of the Orange Free State, John Brand, determined to settle the border problem once and for all. He ordered the Basotho within a month's time to clear out of a portion of the territory which had been awarded the Boers by the Treaty of Aliwal.

Some of the European observers were indignant at the cruelty of the order. The French missionaries had by this time returned to their stations, and the Reverend F. Coillard wrote home to his Church Board of Governors:

> In a country where there are neither railways nor telegraphs, one may well be astonished at the rigor of such a decree, for before Moshoeshoe knew of it, or could assemble the petty chiefs, or these latter could return home and publish the order in the most distant villages, there was very little of this month of grace left. . . .

Pointing out that the natives had already plowed and sowed a crop for the coming year's food, and could not provide themselves with corn for the journey, Coillard continued:

> . . . They suddenly left their villages and took refuge on this side of the Caledon. For days there was nothing but horsemen . . . troops of cattle filling the air with their bellowing; women and children seeking a hole to hide in under the rocks. I saw thousands of women and children wandering shelterless and foodless in the mountains covered with snow.

The following year a bloody struggle broke out. The Boers would accept only two possible outcomes—to drive out the Basotho completely or to break them so that they would become virtual serfs. The Basotho suffered defeats at Berea and Vechtkop, but the Boers were beaten back from Thaba Bosiu. The endless, dreary war was laying waste to the country. Moshoeshoe, understanding that time was on the side of the Boers, again appealed to Governor Wodehouse for British help and the annexation of Basutoland to the British Empire. The British Colonial Office and the Foreign Minister had been considering the matter for years. What was their hurry now? But for Moshoeshoe there was indeed urgency, for his people, crowded on the little land they had left, faced famine.

To obtain peace from the Boers in 1866, he had to sign a humiliating treaty that meant the final loss of one-half of their fertile land. The Basotho were crowded into the Maluti and Drakensburg Mountains. As Moshoeshoe looked out on some of the most spectacular scenery in Africa, he concluded he would have gladly traded all the stark alpine beauty for the return of the lush fields of wheat along the Caledon.

Desperate at the injustices before their eyes, the missionaries began to write letters back home to England and to France, describing the bitter condition of the natives and calling for action by all decent men to right the wrongs they had witnessed. "Natural rights, past grievances, past benefits, past engagements and treaties, feudal allegiances, kindred ties, family bonds, have all been discarded and overlooked," they wrote. The Boers hit back by again expelling the French missionaries in the conquered Basotho territory. This caused an uproar in Europe. Moshoeshoe sent many appeals to the British Foreign Office and to the Prime Minister.

In March of 1868, Moshoeshoe's people at last came "under the Queen's blanket." With the annexation of Basutoland to the Cape Colony, the British insisted that the Boers return some of the lost territory to the tiny nation. Now the People of the Crocodile would be protected from extermination by the Boers.

Moshoeshoe died soon after that in 1870, at the age of 80. Symbolically, his funeral procession was led by the students of Morija High School, an institution which had not even existed at his birth.

Moshoeshoe was a king who began every speech to his people with, "My lords, my masters," a ruler whose humblest subject could come to him at any hour of the day or night and be heard patiently. A realist dealing in practical possibilities, he nevertheless accomplished a political feat that seemed possible only to dreamers. He was so committed to his lofty principles that he used every means, even treachery, to gain his worthy ends.

A British governor described Moshoeshoe as "the most enlightened and upright Chief in South Africa, worthy of perfect confidence and respect." One European historian wrote, "He stands at the parting of the ways between the old and new day in South Africa." And Carter Woodson, American historian, concludes, "the millenium he thought would come, not in the continuation of self-exterminating wars, but in learning from others the best of their culture and to unite with the best in that of Africa."

Today, almost a century later, the land of Moshoeshoe is completely surrounded by South Africa, a country ruled by the descendants of the Boers. The inhuman treatment of the black majority in that nation has been denounced by most of the world, but the white minority refuses to change. The Basotho people, whose tiny land of Lesotho, with fewer than a million people, became proudly independent in 1966, need the goodwill of their overpowering neighbor. About half of the Basotho men, unable to scratch a living from their mountainous soil, work in the gold and diamond mines of South Africa. Those who remain at home live mainly by sheep and cattle raising. The future of Lesotho does not look promising, unless the enormous potential of their mountain streams can be harnessed into hydroelectric energy—a difficult task in the face of Lesotho's poverty. Yet, through the courage and wisdom of Moshoeshoe, his people have the one gift they prize most dearly, their freedom.

Perhaps it is the Basotho themselves who can best sum up the meaning of the life of their beloved chief. When, after an absence, Basotho return to their country, they say, simply, "We are going back to Moshoeshoe."

TOM MBOYA

TOM Mboya recalled December 6, 1958, as the proudest day in his life. Chafing over delays in London, he arrived in Accra airport eighteen hours late for the first All-African Peoples Conference. The broad-shouldered, well-tailored Kenyan was greeted with the news that the 500 delegates representing some 200 million Africans had chosen him chairman of the meeting.

As he entered the hall, Mboya was dazzled by the multi-colored robes and militant posters of the assembled trade unionists, political party workers and other representatives of African groups. They had gathered in newly independent Ghana to plan for the total liberation of Africa from European colonial masters.

Standing under a huge map of the restless continent, the new chairman advised colonialists to "scram from Africa." "What Africans are fighting for is nothing revolutionary," he declared. "It is found in the charter of the United Nations." He also warned the big powers that if they "have nothing better to do than to fight each other, let them do so outside of Africa." "Africa for the Africans!" The auditorium echoed with the thunderous applause and cheers of the delegates. Tom Mboya, the tough-talking twenty-eight-year-old trade union leader from East Africa, had broadcast their message to the world.

Born in 1930, Tom Mboya was the first of five brothers and three sisters. His parents were Luos, whose tribal homelands are in Western Kenya. They had left their native tsetse fly-infested Rusinga Island in Lake Victoria to work on a great sisal plantation in the cool, green highlands near Nairobi. His father, Leonard Ndiege, tall, quiet and popular among his fellow workers, was paid £1, or $2.80, a month by the manager who supervised the estate for an absentee white owner. Marcella Awour, Tom's mother, gave birth to her first son in a typical mud and wattle house with a grass thatch roof and red earth floor stamped hard and smooth by bare feet. Converted to Roman Catholicism by missionaries living on the estate, Leonard and Marcella baptized their son Thomas, but added the name Odhiambo, meaning "evening," which, according to Luo custom, told the time of his birth. Also traditional was a second name after a worthy relative of the mother; Mboya was an uncle, a wise man and a great warrior.

Although they were both illiterate, Tom's parents were determined that their children would have a better life. From his meager earnings the father saved £3 a year for school fees. This was also a good investment for the future, since an educated son would be in a better position to help his parents when they were too old to continue working. The moon-faced, somber-eyed seven-year-old trudged four miles each way to the mission school, where he repeated the catechism and recited prayers daily.

After two years young Tom was sent to the Kabaa School, about twenty-five miles away, to learn to read and write. He lived with one of the teachers in a simple hut without sanitary facilities or running water. A few shillings a month were paid for Tom's food, but the nine-year-old helped around the house in return for his lodging. His lessons at Kabaa were conducted under a tree. There were no books, pencils, blackboards or chalk. Lessons were written on the sand with a stick or fingers.

After three years the missionary fathers sent their promising young pupil to St. Mary's School in the Luo tribal area in Central Nyanza. It was 1942; the trains were overburdened with the demands of a faraway war, and it took three uncomfortable days to travel 300 miles. But for Tom this was high adventure. He mixed easily with people from other tribes and tried to absorb something of their language and customs. When he arrived at St. Mary's, he found work in the priests' kitchens. With his sister and second brother now in school, he had to help defray the £8 a year it cost to keep him in boarding school.

Tom loved the Catholic ritual; for a time he felt a calling for the priesthood and even made application for the seminary. As he matured, however, he began to have doubts. When did the Church ever fight against the English government to help Africans? He talked over his worries with his cousin Peter Otieno, who was also thinking of becoming a priest. If souls have no color in the eyes of God, then why does the Church enforce segregation of races in their schools, in their hospitals, at social affairs and in residences?

"Whenever the question comes up about the future of Africa, what does the Church answer, Peter?"

His cousin thought for a moment, and his features hardened as he firmly answered, "To be patient, to believe in God, that we are not yet ready."

"Exactly," said Tom sharply. "You know some churches preach that it is immoral to give Africans an academic education because the Bible says that black men are cursed always to do the manual labor or dirty jobs. How can we believe that? How long can we be patient? Who decides when we are ready?"

Peter considered the question, but Tom was already off on a new tack. "Our Luo songs and dances . . ."

His cousin interrupted hastily. "The fathers say they are un-civilized. After all, we are here to learn to be cultured men."

Tom grabbed hold of his arm. "But what is their definition of 'cultured'?"

There was a long pause. "To be . . . to be . . . British."

"Well, we have an African culture of our own. Why must we junk everything that is ours in order to be Christian? I've been listening to the priests and thinking about this for a long time. What we need is an Africanization of the Church. The Bible and Church teachings could be interpreted to include our tribal customs and culture." Tom thought for a moment and went on. "The fathers do a lot of good, but I cannot make this my life's work, Peter. I see the Church as an arm of the colonial governments, accepting and spreading the lie of African inferiority, making us fearful, holding us down. I'll change my opinion when I hear a bishop denounce the British government!"

Still undecided about his future, Tom went on to a Catholic high school, Holy Ghost College, located in Kikuyuland near the Aberdare Mountains. Tuition and board amounted to the impos-sible sum of £10 a year, but he was awarded a partial scholarship from the African District Council, which supported bright young men of the Luo tribe, and earned the rest of the money as an aide in the infirmary. There the future labor leader had his first experience as participant in a strike. Disgusted over the inferior food they were served, the students decided one evening to protest by boycotting dinner. Afraid to incur the wrath of the principal, they later said that everyone had stomach trouble. As medical prefect Tom was called upon to verify the boys' illness, and took on himself the unpleasant obligation of telling the principal the truth.

Otherwise, he did not distinguish himself at Holy Ghost. He is remembered as an average student with his nose in books while others took their responsibilities less seriously. He played the flute, sang in the choir and with a Luo folk group, became a Boy Scout patrol leader and joined the debating club.

Each time he visited his parents at the sisal plantation he became more depressed. The oppressively long working day, the absence of safety precautions, the discouraged laborers, with their backs bent from the burdens of years and their skin diseased from the steady drip of water off the sisal, the lack of sanitation—all this made an impression upon Tom's mind and shaped a determination to do something for his people.

His feelings about the Church were reinforced when the missionaries on the plantation denounced educated boys because, they said, they did not respect tradition. "That, translated, means we are not subservient to white men," Tom thought. Before they went into church the visiting scholars were made to rumple their hair and take off their shoes, so that their appearance would be less unusual. "Why should a black man's wish to be neat and well dressed be considered evil?" Tom wondered.

At this time young Mboya's ambition was to go to Makerere College in Uganda, and perhaps study overseas. However, he had to face the immediate problem of earning his own way. His father had tired of the hard work and brutal treatment on the plantation, and decided to retire to their village home on Rusinga Island.

Tom briefly considered becoming a teacher, but he finally chose a career as a sanitary inspector. During training he would receive pocket money, and after passing the qualifying examination he could work anywhere in British-controlled East or Central Africa on an equal basis with Europeans and Asians.

So, in 1948, Tom entered the Royal Sanitary Institute Medical School. He was a plump, awkward young man of eighteen, dressed in the standard khaki uniform, his socks falling down around his fat calves. He studied anatomy, elementary physics, water and drainage problems, sewage and garbage disposal, ventilation and carpentry. The classes learned firsthand by weekly practice in meat inspection at the Nairobi slaughterhouse and spot checks of eggs and vegetables at the city markets. Here again Tom noticed the kind of bias which was coming to offend him more and more sharply—the identification of high-quality maize or eggs as "European-grade" and all inferior produce as "African-grade."

Since he was never an outstanding student, Tom's energies and attention became caught up in politics. He argued with his classmates, slipped away to Nairobi to attend meetings, read about Abraham Lincoln and Booker T. Washington. Within a few months he was President of the Student Council at Jeanes School, where the Royal Institute was housed.

As leader of 1,000 students Tom presided over meetings, supervised correspondence and publicity, met with the principal and the staff, checked to see that all school-sponsored organizations were functioning well and participated in decisions on spending school funds. The headmaster encouraged students to run their own affairs as much as possible, but a new principal arrived with ideas of his own. When he tried to cut down the powers of the Student Council, Tom resigned in protest. In later life, he recalled those two years of student leadership as excellent experience for his adult responsibilities.

In January, 1951, Mboya qualified as a sanitary inspector and went to work for the Nairobi City Council. Here, for the first time, racial prejudice hit him full-on. He told of an incident which occurred in the Health Department food section while one of his European fellow workers was away on leave. He was busy testing milk samples to make sure they conformed to standards and were free from disease when a white woman came in with a sample bottle of milk. She looked around and seemed unsure of what to do.

"Good morning, madam," Mboya greeted her cordially.

She looked at him and asked, "Is there anybody here?"

His first reaction was shock and anger, but he then decided that the situation was amusing. "Is there something wrong with your eyes?" he asked.

She became beet-red with fury, and the next day she brought a petition she had persuaded other European farmers to sign, stating that they insisted on a white inspector and would not deal with an African. Mboya's chief stood by him and informed the woman that, if she wanted her license, she would have to deal with whichever inspector was available. Later he tried to soothe Mboya's feelings, while sadly warning him that such incidents were to be expected.

Instances of racial prejudice became an everyday routine. To gain experience, Mboya was teamed with a European inspector. As they made the rounds, the young African was left to sit in the car while the white made certain calls. When he realized that these were homes that would not admit a black to inspect the premises, he registered a strong protest. Later, when he was on his own, he was thrown off the premises by some Europeans, but it is to the credit of the City Council that they took these people into court for interfering with an inspector.

In these incidents the British authorities were behind him, but against other kinds of treatment Mboya found no recourse. African inspectors were paid one-fifth the salary of the Europeans for doing the same job. African inspectors were ordered to wear khaki uniforms while white inspectors wore ordinary business clothing.

As Mboya fought for equality it was inevitable that he would move into the leadership of the Staff Association, which functioned as a kind of union.

Many of the low-paid menial workers who were illiterate or spoke poorly turned to him with their grievances—errors in wage payments or sick pay, unjust working conditions or delays in promised housing. Mboya spent much of his time talking to their European bosses, who were unaware of or had simply ignored many injustices.

As he moved around Nairobi on his sanitary inspections, he became ever more conscious of the contrast between the dusty, dirty, cramped, ugly black locations and the flowering gardens and neat lawns of the luxurious European areas. He saw his activities in the sanitation workers' Staff Association as a practical, positive way he could help his people progress.

One day Mboya was introduced to James Patrick, a Scotsman who had been sent by the British Labour Party to encourage trade unionism in the colonies. Patrick had vast experience in organizing unions, setting up negotiating machinery, advising employers on dealing with labor matters and helping to plan legal procedures for the government to follow. He felt frustrated at every turn in Kenya. The whites had told him in so many words: "Come back in twenty years." However, an eager Tom Mboya adopted Patrick as his mentor. The young man attended courses for trade unionists, borrowed books and explored new ideas in long discussions.

Before long, Mboya made contact with the staff associations of sanitary workers in the main towns of Kenya. He traveled to Mombasa, Nakuru, Kisumu and Eldoret, and everywhere he received a cordial welcome from many of his former classmates from the Jeanes School. His aim was to put together all the local staff associations into a Kenya-wide Local Government Workers Union. Drawing on his experience as head of the Student Council, he built a tough, well-organized labor association with an efficient office staff and the largest bank account of any African union. From

450 registrants when Mboya became general secretary, the Kenya Local Government Workers Union in eight months grew to 1,321 paid-up members.

While the twenty-two-year-old Mboya was busy arguing for union recognition, negotiating on behalf of the workers and organizing squads of women to collect dues, Kenya exploded into terrorism and violence. From the countryside came an increasing number of strange reports—houses had been burned, cattle or other animals had been slashed and left as ominous warnings on the doorsteps of white farmers, corpses had been found weirdly mutilated. There were frightening rumors of revolting ceremonies featuring black magic among the Kikuyu, Kenya's largest tribal group. It was said that members of the Mau Mau secret society were bound by blood-curdling oaths against the whites and against all other Kikuyus who did not join the struggle to liberate Kenya. Brutal intimidation kept those Kikuyus who wavered in line. The entire world was horrified by stories of Europeans hacked to death by trusted servants, women strangled and dismembered, white families abandoning their farms and fleeing in terror. These racial atrocities were sensational news, but far less publicized was the fact that an estimated ninety-five Europeans, only thirty-two of whom were civilians, were killed, while 2,356 Africans, 1,832 of them civilians, died during the Mau Mau rebellion.

Since Tom Mboya was of the Luo tribe, he was not personally involved in the uprising, but he sought to understand its causes. At a meeting of the Kenya African Union he first saw Jomo Kenyatta, a tall, powerfully built, middle-aged man in old corduroy trousers, sitting quietly as the noisy gathering sang hymns in his praise and danced wildly in the aisles. When he arose to speak, the crowd roared and the Kikuyu women in their bright kerchiefs pierced the din with ululating screams of delight. Waving a carved elephant stick, Kenyatta began softly, "My brothers, my sisters. . ."

But when he spoke of the British injustices, his voice became aggressive and challenging. He reminded the packed audience of their constant degradation by the whites—of the hated passes they had to carry and present on demand, of their tribal lands in the highlands stolen by Europeans, of the severe overcrowding in the tribal reserves, of the unequal wages for similar work; of the restricted educational opportunities and of the ugly, unsanitary, unsafe housing in the African quarters in the cities.

Kenyatta refused to condemn the Mau Mau. To him, as well as to many other Africans, they were "freedom fighters" whose methods might be unpleasant, but who might very well force England into granting some fundamental human rights to the blacks of Kenya.

On October 20, 1952, a state of emergency was declared and many African leaders were rounded up in a wave of arrests. Kenyatta was one of them, but even after his trial and conviction for leading the Mau Mau revolt, Mboya believed that the nationalist leader was being made "a scapegoat of a desperate colonial government."

Mboya was outraged at the way in which the British had acted. "I cannot support the violence of the Mau Mau," he stated, "but the government policy of meeting violence with violence is wrong. They would do better to root out the economic and social grievances out of which the Mau Mau terrorism grows."

Like many educated Africans he vowed never to forget Jomo Kenyatta as a symbol of Africa's future, and threw himself into the struggle for justice in a land torn by a small civil war and atrocities on both sides. His first step was to take out formal membership in the Kenya African Union. His father and other elders in the tribe warned him, "We can never compete with the European. After all, he has airplanes, he flies about while we walk on foot. He has cars and he has guns. Can we compete with the white man when we don't yet know how to make a nail?"

"Freedom has nothing to do with riches or schooling or civilization," the young labor leader answered. "Europeans have not understood the meaning of African nationalism and objectives of African leaders. If the whites make no concessions to reasonable African ambitions and feelings, if they block every peaceful approach, then they should not be surprised that the African turns to bloodshed."

Mboya wrote for *Habari za Dunia* (*News of the World*), a Swahili-language newspaper, and helped people understand the issues with a flood of political pamphlets listing grievances and demanding the return of the land. Soon his political activities came to the notice of his employers, the Nairobi City Council. Anticipating dismissal from his job, Mboya gave notice that he was resigning. However, before the customary three months were up, his employers requested the militant sanitary worker to leave. This was quite a financial blow to the young man, who had acquired a taste for clothes, automobiles and good living after his long childhood deprivation.

In addition, the declaration of martial law by the British government almost destroyed the Kenya Local Government Workers Union. The movements of Kikuyu and certain other tribesmen were severely restricted. Union headquarters were raided and officers arrested. During the frequent house checks and roadblock searches, anyone found carrying a union card was considered a hard-core subversive and shipped off to detention camp. Mboya himself was trailed by detectives, and from time to time his living quarters were searched for incriminating evidence. To foil the police, he moved from one friend's house to another, lugging about with him a large wicker clothes basket in which he kept union funds to prevent them from being taken over by the government. He lived on donations from friends.

The political situation worsened as the experienced African leaders were rounded up. Tom Mboya was sucked into the leadership vacuum, and after a short time moved into the post of treasurer. It took great courage to become a leader of the Kenya African Union in 1952. On the one side the party was being infiltrated by fanatical Mau Maus who would stop at nothing; on the other stood the threat of the government police force. However, even his most bitter enemies have never accused Mboya of a lack of courage.

He did not function as treasurer for very long, because in June 1953 the Kenya African Union and all other political parties were banned. If he could not fight for his people through a political party, he decided, he would work through the labor movement. The Kenya Federation of Labour was the only organized group of Africans not yet banned because of the Mau Mau emergency. "It will have to take over as the voice of the African people," Mboya decided.

The Kenya Federation of Labour protested the mass eviction of the Kikuyu, Embu and Meru tribes from Rift Valley Province on suspicion of taking part in hideous Mau Mau oaths. This area was their traditional homeland, and they had no way of making a living elsewhere. In the same year 700 families were thrown out of their homes and into the streets of the Eastleigh suburb of Nairobi.

Mboya publicly raged against the passbook requirements, confiscation of cattle and other property of detained Africans and collective punishments where the innocent were heavily fined along with those guilty of anti-British acts. When a boycott was organized among Nairobi's black people against buses, beer and cigarettes, the District Commissioner called on Mboya to condemn the protestors. He angrily refused. "I am not responsible for the conditions which created the boycott," he said.

By now the young labor leader had risen to be general secretary of the Kenya Federation of Labour, and he sent an SOS overseas to other labor organizations, older and more experienced in political action. The International Confederation of Free Trade Unions not only sent representatives to help the KFL, but money to feed evicted African families. Their lawyers also presented the African side of the Kenya story to the International Labor Organization of the United Nations, made strong protests to the British Colonial Office in London and brought pressure on various members of Parliament. To counteract news out of Kenya that dwelled only on Mau Mau atrocities, Tom Mboya wrote in *Free Labor World* and other international publications. He tried to rally world opinion against drastic British countermeasures by publicizing such things as the bonus offered to security forces if they "shot straight and shot an African" and the case of Peter Evans, a Nairobi lawyer who was deported when he uncovered evidence of police brutality and demanded an investigation. Jim Bury, a Canadian ICFTU adviser to the Kenya Federation of Labour, was threatened with expulsion from Kenya several times, and the KFL itself would probably have been banned except for the intervention of Sir Vincent Tewson of the British Trades Union Congress.

On April 24, 1954, began Operation Anvil, the biggest of British police actions and one which gave Mboya a personal taste of the bitter fruit of the Mau Mau Emergency. After most Africans in Nairobi were already at work one morning, truckloads of soldiers suddenly appeared and sealed off certain areas with machine guns. Mboya ran out of his office to see what was happening, but within seconds he was challenged by a soldier, shoved with a gun butt and ordered to squat down with other Africans. Some had paint marks on their faces, and Mboya learned that these were people who were found in suspicious circumstances or who had not stopped or obeyed the soldiers' orders quickly enough. They remained squatting in this way for several hours. It began to rain, and Tom sensed the terror of these people facing the ordeal of an interrogation. They had all heard of being herded into a room where government informers, wearing hoods to protect their identity, could condemn them simply by pointing at them. There was no trial, no witnesses, no face-to-face confrontation. It was up to the accused to prove his innocence without the benefit of a lawyer.

At last they were packed into trucks and driven to a "reception" camp ringed round with barbed wire barriers. Again they had to squat in the dust for hours. Finally, they were ordered to rise and line up according to tribe. All non-Kikuyus were marched to the barbed-wire enclosure and told, "You are free to leave, but do not go back to the cordoned area where you were picked up this morning."

Despite his relief at being set free without charges, Tom turned back to look at the others. His face hardened with anger at the thought that, for the British, the simple fact of belonging to the Kikuyu tribe was enough proof of Mau Mau sympathies.

When he returned to Nairobi, Mboya found that Operation Anvil had smashed the Kenya Federation of Labour to pieces. A group of union officials had been meeting in the office when two European police officers had hammered at the door and immediately fired through a cardboard partition. One of the men was shot in the hip and was rushed to a hospital. There, without inquiry, he was classified as a terrorist and would have been sent away but for strong KFL protests. Thirty-nine other labor officials were arrested, and only after two months of constant pressure did the Ministry of Labour intervene to order a rescreening of the charges against them. In one day Mboya found that membership in the Kenya Local Government Workers Union was reduced from 1,300 to 500. "There was no one left to run the offices and carry on," he later recalled.

In the midst of frenzied activities to rebuild his union base and pursue his editorial work on the *News of the World*, Mboya in mid-1954 saw a chance to travel and try to influence world opinion on events in Kenya. He visited the headquarters of the International Confederation of Free Trade Unions in Brussels, Belgium, and the International Labor Organization in Geneva, Switzerland. In London, officials at the British Trades Union Congress welcomed the twenty-four-year-old African, who found it hard to keep his sense of direction in the bustling, noisy city. In November he and Jim Bury attended an ICTFU International Seminar in Calcutta, India, on worker education in economically undeveloped countries. From there they went to Karachi, Pakistan, and then back to Africa for a conference of the Commission for Technical Cooperation South of the Sahara which met in Beira, Mozambique. Bury received many favorable comments from other delegates on the brilliant logic and excellent English expression of his young protégé. At these international meetings Mboya worked tirelessly, spending little time visiting landmarks or inquiring about local customs. What interested Tom were ideas, policies and people.

Not long after they returned to Kenya, Mboya and Bury got an urgent call from Mombasa, steaming port city on the Indian Ocean. There dock workers, smoldering under their many grievances, driven to desperation by grinding poverty, had thrown out their elected union officials and called a wildcat strike. Mboya had played a part in starting the Dock Workers Union some years before, but he was not in sympathy with this strike. "Calling a strike is easy; but stopping it, getting things back to normal and winning the negotiations with the bosses—that's the real test," he told the workers. "The job of a labor leader is not to call strikes but to gain improvements. You have to negotiate anyhow. Don't make unneeded suffering. Work while the meetings are going on."

The answer of the wildcat strikers was a riot. Stones were thrown at cars, buses and trucks, a policeman was injured and many demonstrators were arrested. Crudely lettered signs in Swahili were posted around the docks: "Anyone who works will die." The Asian-owned shops all through Mombasa were dark behind locked doors and shuttered windows. A mass meeting of dock workers was scheduled at Tononoka football stadium that afternoon. Police were planning to move in the dreaded General Service Unit and follow up with the Army if the threatening situation continued.

Tom requested permission from the Provincial Commissioner and the Coast Province Security Committee to address the rally without any troops or police present. One white reporter who did not know that whites were excluded was set upon by the crowd. "Get him into our car before he gets torn to pieces," Mboya shouted to an aide. To the menacing crowd of about 10,000 he yelled, "We must stop this! WE MUST STOP THIS! I insisted that no police be at this meeting to show them we can look after our own affairs. This just gives them a chance to say we are still incapable."

This was the first mass meeting Mboya had ever addressed. As he looked over the tough audience—powerfully muscled men in tattered shirts, illiterate and crude, but determined to carry through their fight—the twenty-five-year-old wondered if he were equal to the task. The young man began hesitatingly, but soon his passionate Swahili began to seep into their minds. His persuasive voice hypnotized them. For several hours he worked his oral magic, sympathizing, reasoning, cajoling, advising. Just as he felt he was near his goal—asking the dockers to vote to return to work while a court commission investigated their complaints—the employers showered the stadium with leaflets. Strikers would either return to the docks or be dismissed, read their message. The meeting broke up in cursing and disorder.

Mboya went straight to the government representatives and the employers. "Unless that ultimatum is withdrawn," he told them, "I can do nothing to help." The next day they complied with his demand.

Then he sought out the leaders to whom the desperate dock workers had turned. In the mud-plastered huts with their rusting iron roofs, on the stinking docks piled high with rotting cargo, Mboya talked quietly to small groups. He also listened carefully. They had heard him at the meeting and trusted and admired him. On the third day the men went back to work and hearings began. The law provided that the workers could have a lawyer. Tom Mboya became the dockers' advocate, assisted by Bury and Mrs. Meta Peel, a Labour Office Secretary. Four weeks later he emerged with a 33 per cent increase in wages and the genuine admiration of both bosses and workers. Immediately afterward he drew up ground rules for a Joint Industrial Council which provided ways for employers and employees to settle their differences peacefully without strikes. "We are dealing with a new breed of African," one white businessman said.

A month later Mboya savored a new triumph. For two years the demands of the Kenya Local Government Workers Union for recognition as the bargaining agent for sanitary workers had been dragging. Finally a Board of Inquiry under Mr. Justice Windham

was called. Mboya made a four-hour presentation of the workers'
case. Mayor Reggie Alexander of Nairobi stood firm against
recognition. The judge's report later praised "the reasonable and
patient attitude adopted by the Nairobi branch of the KLGWU . . .
its efficiency of organization, including bookkeeping, and its reasonable and cooperative manner of presentation."

Tom Mboya was a young man who was ambitious and dedicated
to the improvement of his people. He was doing well on both
counts by mid-1955, when he was offered an unusual chance—a year
at Oxford University in England to study industrial relations and
political institutions. The Kenya government offered £150 ($420)
toward his expenses, and the British Trades Union Congress arranged for a scholarship to cover the rest of the cost. Still regretful
over his lack of university training, Mboya seized on the opportunity to read, reflect and meet scholars and thinkers from all over the
world.

In Oxford, he settled in a hostel in a converted old country
house, and soon became secretary of one of the college student
bodies and joined the Oxford University Labour and Socialist
Clubs. Back in Kenya he had been barred from European circles
by his color and had met but few African intellectuals, so he found
the atmosphere at Oxford intoxicating. He drank in the ideas, the
thoughts, the brilliant conversations. With British Labour Party
people, other trade unionists and fellow students he talked, de-
bated and discussed far into the night.

Mboya was in great demand for seminars, speeches and discussion groups, and at one of these, in Nuffield College, he met
Margery Perham, one of the world's most prominent scholars and
authors on African affairs.

"Nobody has written about these things," she encouraged him.
"The African point of view is unknown. Why don't you write
something about it?" Eventually Tom's pamphlet called *The Kenya
Question, an African Answer* was published by the Fabian Society,
and Miss Perham wrote the foreword. Long after he left Oxford,
Mboya maintained a detailed correspondence with the aging Af-

ricanist, testing out his ideas against her knowledgeable, critical, compassionate mind.

Some observers who knew him in Nairobi were surprised that he did not lead more of a social life in England. As a young government worker he had loved gay parties, dancing and pretty girls. One biographer states that Mboya had become very attached to a girl whom he would never marry because she was white and would handicap his rise in African politics.

Mboya himself summed up his year at Oxford this way: ". . . When I look back today, I feel that Oxford played a major part in my life, giving me a year of unhurried thought to help me decide what line of policies would be effective in our struggle. The year at Oxford gave me more confidence in myself, it gave me the time to read more, it taught me to look to books as a source of knowledge. It led me to take part in intellectual discussions, sometimes of a very provocative nature, and it helped me to think more analytically about problems and work out on paper how best to meet them."

Before returning to Kenya, Mboya made the first of many visits to the United States. Under the sponsorship of the American Committee on Africa he toured the country, appearing on television and radio, meeting with individuals and representatives of organizations interested in Africa. Many Americans were impressed with the vigorous, well-dressed young man who spoke Oxford English with a soft accent, and he greatly stimulated American interest in Africa. The twenty-six-year-old labor leader solicited a gift of $35,000 from the AFL-CIO to build a new headquarters for the Kenya Federation of Labour. It was during his tour that he first heard that scholarships set aside for Africans were not being used because of the prohibitively expensive air fare. He discussed the problem with executive board member William Scheinman of the American Committee on Africa, a manufacturer of hydraulic components for aircraft, and the businessman offered to pay for seventeen scholars in 1957. In 1958 he picked up the bill for thirty-six students, but it was obvious that some more systematic method had to be found than relying on Mr. Scheinman's generosity.

When he flew into Nairobi in November, 1956, after thirteen months abroad, Mboya was rudely reminded that the emergency still existed in Kenya and that he was once more a black man in a land ruled by white colonialists. Forty policemen were on duty, and Tom watched with a sardonic smile as customs officials combed through his luggage searching for seditious literature. "Of course they could find nothing," he said to his companions as they drove toward the city. "They didn't know where to look." He pointed to his head. "It's all up here."

Hardly had Mboya settled into his tiny apartment when he was besieged by supporters demanding that he run for the Legislative Council in the March, 1957, election. Up to then a few blacks had been appointed to the Legislative Council, but now, for the first time since the Kenya African Union was banned, the government allowed political parties to be organized on a local basis, and some Africans would be elected. Mboya was undecided. He felt that the Kenya Federation of Labour had made some wrong decisions under the leadership of Arthur Ochwada, another ambitious young man who was his rival, and he was eager to take over his old job of general secretary. He also felt that the British were making a mockery of democracy in the forthcoming election. He believed in "one man, one vote," and he was very much against the so-called fancy franchise which the British had enacted: in order to vote, an African had to be over twenty-one and have one of seven qualifications—an income of £120 a year; long service in the army, government or police; membership in a local government authority; a certificate or medal for meritorious service; or a long, favorable employment record in agriculture or industry. Under this system well-qualified Africans could have up to three votes.

"Perhaps some 400,000 new voters will be added to the election rolls," Tom said to a visitor from England, "but what about the millions of Kenyans still disenfranchised? The government has made certain that only the most conservative vote. The real fighters haven't got a chance to cast a ballot."

The visitor from England was Aneurin Bevan, a fiery Labour Party politician. "You would be a fool to boycott the elections," he told Mboya bluntly. "You have to be realistic when you're in a struggle for political power. Even if Africans are offered only one seat in the Legislative Council, grab it. Then use it as a forum to broadcast your demands. The British people believe in fair play. Back home they will soon begin to realize that five million people are unfairly represented in Kenya as compared with 50,000 whites. Even if it's insulting and humiliating, take what's offered. Use it as a steppingstone. Keep pressing for more."

Mboya gave a green light to his followers, who formed the Nairobi People's Convention Party. Soon he was taken up in a frenzy of organizing election committees, collecting funds and making speeches. His opponent was Clement A. Khodeck, a lawyer who had his degree from the University of Wales and who had gained much popularity because he had been fighting the cases of Kikuyus charged with taking Mau Mau oaths.

The fever-pitch campaign which followed had its amusing moments. Mboya's People's Convention Party had drawn from a hat its election symbol of a cock; Khodeck's Nairobi African District Congress had selected a lion. All over Nairobi the badges of each candidate appeared on clothing tags and posters. When they spotted an opponent, Mboya's supporters threw back their brightly kerchiefed heads and crowed like a cock. Khodeck's supporters growled back at them like lions. At a rally a Khodeck supporter shouted, "How could you vote for jogoo [a cock]? It can be eaten by a lion!" But a sharp-witted Mboya aide replied, "It is an African custom never to set up a new house without a cockerel. Kenya is our new home, for we are going into the Legislative Council for the first time. Do you trust a lion as an animal to have around the house? You never know when it will become hungry and eat you up!"

As in every hard-fought political campaign, there was also a good deal of rumor and malicious talk. "At twenty-six Tom Mboya is too young," it was said. "Youth provides revolutionary fervor," he answered. "He's unmarried," they said. "A wife doesn't enter into debates in the Legislative Council," was his reply. "He has no university degree." "Winston Churchill and quite a few U.S. presidents did without it," Mboya countered.

"Look at him," they said. "His face is impassive; he's always thinking, scheming. He's a mind without a heart. He's suspicious; he trusts no one. He'll sacrifice anyone to his political ambitions."

But there were enough voters in Nairobi who had seen another side of Tom Mboya—a charming, warm, humorous, generous young man. "Perhaps it is true," they said, "that people are not as important to him as goals. But his goals are our goals—political freedom, human dignity, economic opportunity." They remembered that he was born poor and underprivileged, just like most of them, and that now he could match any white. On March 10, 1957, he was the first African declared elected to the Legislative Council.

When the other results were announced, Mboya sent telegrams of congratulations to all the winners and invited them to come to Nairobi for a meeting to plan joint strategy. In his first press statement Mboya declared, "Public meetings have been forbidden; African leaders are in jail or banished. The Constitution was imposed on us and is therefore null and void."

The African elected representatives launched Operation Freedom, a five-year program to desegregate schools and other public places, extend voting rights to all adults and break the white monopoly on property in the highlands. They refused to accept appointments as ministers in the new government until they had a new constitution which gave Africans the majority of seats to which they were entitled by population. When moderate Europeans expressed shock at his intransigence, Mboya replied, "Why should we take responsibility for carrying out orders of a colonial government?"

On his first day in the Legislative Council, Mboya wore a new suit and, flashing his famous grin, he took his place on the front bench of the nongovernment side of the chamber. His first action was to introduce a vote of no confidence in the Kenya government. Mboya knew it could never carry, but he counted on widespread press coverage to dramatize their demands for the release of Jomo Kenyatta and other prisoners, and the removal of the ban on meetings and other curbs of African civil liberties. Then motion after motion was introduced by the Africans—end the emergency, restore freedom of assembly, allow the present system of local political parties to expand on a national basis and end social discrimination. In each case, the Africans were monotonously snowed under by votes of the white legislators.

Mboya also noted that if an Englishman made a speech to fifteen whites, however inconsequential, he received front-page coverage in the European-controlled newspapers. If an African addressed 10,000 at a mass rally, it was written up in a small corner of an inside page. Accordingly, his People's Convention Party began its own newspaper named *Uhuru*, the Swahili word for freedom.

Seven months of determined action by Mboya and the other Africans in the Legislative Council brought the British Colonial Secretary Alan Lennox-Boyd to Kenya to discuss an increase in African representation. He was "strongheaded," Mboya noted, and "difficult to argue with." The Africans pushed for nothing less than freedom. "If it is a bus ride we are invited to join," Mboya told Lennox-Boyd, "let us have in clear terms the destination, for unless we are agreed on this we shall certainly not agree as to the route."

After much argument, the Africans accepted six additional seats in the Legislative Council and determined to continue their pressure. Thus was established a pattern which the Africans followed until they won their independence in 1963. Sometimes the African leaders stood together in their opposition to the British, and sometimes they fought each other because they could not agree on the best course of action or because they were jealous of each other, but their goals were identical: "Uhuru sasa na Kenyatta"—"Freedom now and Kenyatta."

The rest of 1958 was a busy time for Mboya. In September, nationalist leaders from all over East Africa met to coordinate their struggle for freedom. In October, Mboya's role as Chairman of the International Confederation of Free Trade Unions for east, central and southern Africa took him to Ethiopia. There, dressed in a white dinner jacket, he dined with Emperor Haile Selassie and discussed ways to encourage trade unionism in Ethiopia.

At about this time a sensational story fell into Tom Mboya's lap. Rawson Macharia, a supposed eyewitness who had testified against Jomo Kenyatta at his trial, confessed that his story had been false. For several weeks Macharia had offered the scoop to different newspapers, but they were afraid to break the news. Macharia appeared to be unstable, and the disclosure was political dynamite. Eventually, Mboya heard the rumors and arranged a meeting with the confessed perjurer. Macharia signed a complete statement, and Mboya took the new evidence to London to demand Kenyatta's release from his lonely exile in the desert.

From London he flew to Ghana for the All-African People's Congress, which he considered one of the high spots in his life. After Mboya's "Hands off Africa" speech he was given celebrity treatment by Ghana President Kwame Nkrumah and taken to see all that the country had achieved in its first year of independence.

He returned to Kenya greatly impressed. Black Africa was on the march! It could not be long before Kenya threw off its British masters and, like Ghana, could begin to forge its own destiny. "You clap and cheer," he cautioned an exuberant crowd, "but freedom will not come by clapping and cheering, will it? *Uhuru* will only come by hard work, unity and sacrifice. The African people of Kenya are awake and do not intend to sleep anymore."

The police were not asleep either. In the early hours of the morning of March 6, 1959, they hammered at Mboya's door. While he sat watching them in red-eyed disbelief, they went through his drawers, shelves and cupboards. They peered under slip covers and even inspected the outhouse. At the same time, officers and members of the People's Convention Party were arrested all over

Kenya. Omolo Agar, Organizational Secretary of PCP, was convicted of subversive activity on the basis of notes he had made as a student in India three years before. Party Propaganda Secretary J. M. Oyangi was convicted largely on a report which had been sent to him from the 1957 Afro-Asian People's Conference. Of the thirty-nine Africans arrested that night, almost all were PCP leaders.

No charges were pressed against Mboya, although any one of his frequent speeches against the government could have been used as evidence. However, the British did not want to make him a martyr or a symbol, such as Jomo Kenyatta had become. As a result, he was free to make a triumphal tour of the U.S. in the spring of 1959.

In three weeks he gave about one hundred lectures in auditoriums packed to capacity. He spoke in New York, Washington, Boston, Philadelphia, Pittsburgh, Detroit, Chicago, Minneapolis, San Francisco, Los Angeles and Miami, and made frequent TV and radio appearances. He also found time to grant many newspaper interviews to remind Americans that "today's needs call for a rededication to those principles that drove your ancestors to fight for freedom, human rights and justice. Maybe these words have ceased to have a meaning because you have had so much of them that you take them for granted, and have forgotten that there are millions of people throughout the world who don't know the meaning of prosperity, who have never seen a pair of shoes in their lives or even a blanket. . . . We are fighting for political freedom, for economic opportunity and for human dignity. We believe that you stand for the same thing."

In his U.S. travels Mboya met many Afro-Americans, and he reached the conclusion that most American Negroes had lost touch with whatever was African in their background. "Their only knowledge of Africa is from garish films and sensational novels." Only during the last few years, he pointed out, had they seen the flags of Africa flying high and Africans honored in the United Nations, so they could see there was something in their African heritage of which to be proud. However, he felt that the American Negro could not adopt African tribal and other cultural values. "The Negro is as much American as the White American," he concluded.

Mboya liked the United States. It was not only Harry Belafonte records, electric shavers, "fantastic" Miami Beach and dictaphones which delighted him, but also the friendliness and generosity of Americans. He resumed his acquaintance with William Scheinman and worked out a program of chartering planes to reduce costs for African students bound for study in the U.S.

Several months later Mboya was to enjoy the fruits of his efforts. Eighty-one students gathered in Nairobi airport, depositing their luggage and nervously checking through their documents. All the African members of the Legislative Council came—most of them with colorful tribal garments, ceremonial fly-whisks or staffs and beaded caps. While they greeted the families and made introductions, Tom thought of the great sacrifices many students and their families had made to raise the $600 they needed for a three-year stay in the United States. That sum represented borrowing from parents, friends and relatives, petitioning district councils for loans and begging in the street or knocking on strange doors. But now was a time of joy.

At length Mboya climbed the steps of the airplane and announced that forty other students would join them later. As compared with the 120 overseas scholarships arranged by Mboya, the Kenya government gave thirty-two that year. By 1961, 800 Kenyan students were studying in the United States as a result of Mboya's efforts, as well as hundreds of others from east and central Africa. In his speech of farewell, Mboya reminded the students that they were the hope of the new Kenya and ended with the rallying cry "*Uhuru!*"

Mboya was accused of being a black racist by the European-owned newspapers. Some members of the Legislative Council— white, Arab, Asian and black—found that they were able to work together so well that they formed a nonracial political party, the Kenya National Party, whose commendable goal was to work for a free, democratically governed Kenya. Mboya heaped scorn on their efforts, reminding them that Africans still could not have Kenya-wide organizations and that political parties and all other groups were limited to a particular locality. "Africans must have the right to organize on a national basis before we will work with other races," he said. He also faced the whites and Asians with the unavoidable fact that they would be a small minority of the population in an independent Kenya and their political power would be limited accordingly.

Mboya was attacked in the "white press" and by his own African colleagues, but he was practical politician enough to realize that multi-racialism had no future at that stage of the fight for independence. Not long after, the founders of the Kenya National Party found themselves quarreling. As Mboya had predicted, the Africans found they could not lead their people's fight and cooperate with other races at the same time. The party crumbled.

New elections in England had resulted in the appointment of a new Colonial Secretary, Ian Macleod, and early in 1960 he called a conference in London to discuss the future of Kenya. A fierce struggle developed between Mboya and a fellow Luo Legislative Council member, Oginga-Odinga, for leadership of the African delegation. Ronald Ngala was agreed upon as a compromise candidate, and Mboya was designated secretary.

In the elegance of the British government's Lancaster House, beneath crystal chandeliers and gilded ceilings, the Africans made their first demands. They insisted on the presence of two advisers —Peter Mbiu Koinange, an associate of Jomo Kenyatta in the 1940s, and Thurgood Marshall, then counsel for the National Association for the Advancement of Colored People in the United States and now an associate justice of the U.S. Supreme Court. It was pointed out to the Africans that Koinange had small value as an adviser since he had not been in Kenya for many years, but the Africans had reasons of their own. He was a symbol, a stand-in for the man they thought should be the real leader of the delegation, Jomo Kenyatta, still languishing in a remote part of Kenya.

Macleod proved to be a shrewd mixture of compromise and

toughness. He worked out a face-saving way for the Africans to have their advisers present and opened the proceedings with a statement that on independence England would turn Kenya over to be run by its black majority. But the discussion as to just how this would be accomplished inevitably bogged down in bitter disagreement. Macleod worked behind the scenes, charming the delegates, wearing them down, coaxing them and listening patiently to their objections. Finally, he called in the delegates one by one. He told them his formula for a new Constitution for Kenya and asked if they approved or disapproved. When he had seen each one, he announced that the proposal had been rejected by the blacks.

"Very well, gentlemen," he said. "I abide by your decision. I will withdraw my proposals. Within six months I will send a commission to Kenya to hold inquiries. You cannot expect, with so much for them to investigate, that they will make their report before a year."

Macleod knew that his implied threat of a deliberate stall would shake up the Africans. They realized all too well that colonial governments had often avoided unpleasant demands by "unavoidable delays." Tom Mboya advised his colleagues to "tolerate" the Macleod Constitutional proposal as "an instrument which will be used to further our steps toward independence." Perhaps he was thinking of the advice which Aneurin Bevan had once given him.

The African delegation went back to Kenya having accomplished another great step toward independence, but Mboya returned with a heavy heart. It was increasingly evident that his colleagues were joining forces to destroy him politically. Because of his previous visits to England and the United States, Mboya was well known and respected by the newspapers, radio and television reporters. In their pictures and stories he was treated as the effective head of the African delegation, and this caused great jealousy among the others. With Kenya on the brink of independence, all black politicians were jockeying for position. They knew that some would be remembered as founding fathers; others' reputations would crumble in the dust of history.

Oginga-Odinga felt that as a fellow Luo tribesman, Mboya should defer to him because he was older. Ngala charged that Mboya was impossible to work with. One newspaper quoted Masindi Muliro: "It is common knowledge in Kenya politics that Mr. Mboya is the only African politician who is ambitious and will never accept second place in any organization." Others said he was arrogant, domineering and insensitive to the feelings of other people. Ugly rumors of mismanagement of public funds and details of his personal life began to circulate in the bars, dance halls and other meetingplaces in African locations.

Many of the younger, educated clique within the party turned on Mboya. They called themselves the Ginger Group, and their aim was to force a more militant policy—to "ginger things up." Many were young men in a hurry, irritated to find their way up the political ladder blocked by an equally young man who did not have the coveted degree from an overseas university. Mboya had spent his "university years" leading the struggle in Kenya, and now he had political seniority.

It was an open secret that Oginga-Odinga was being financed by the Communist countries and the United Arab Republic. Dressed in traditional Luo garments, Oginga-Odinga related well to people, and his warm personality and fiery nationalism won him many dedicated followers from among Mboya's former friends. Silently, Tom Mboya watched his political future seemingly slip through his fingers.

In March, 1960, Oginga-Odinga announced the formation of the Uhuru Party. He approached each African member of the Legislative Council to join, and then went to all of Mboya's rivals and invited their participation. Few knew that the aim was to freeze out Mboya. When they realized they were being used in a personal vendetta, many withdrew.

His old rival Clement Khodeck charged that Mboya was getting large sums of money from the United States. Another whispered story charged that Mboya had made a secret agreement with British Colonial Secretary Macleod to keep Jomo Kenyatta in prison and to sell out on Kenyan independence. Despite Mboya's record, people seemed too ready to believe the slanders. He could no longer ignore them and called on anyone with proof to make a public charge where he could refute it. No one accepted his challenge.

The final decision on Tom Mboya's future was made at the polls early in 1961 when, in accordance with the Macleod Constitution they had accepted in London the previous year, an election was held for representatives in the first Kenya Legislative Council with an African majority. Mboya's Nairobi constituency turned out in record numbers to reaffirm their faith in his leadership. To the urban worker he was still a fighter for labor's rights, a man who had never stopped pushing for Kenyatta's release, a leader who stood on principle and would not bow down to British colonialists and a representative they were proud to have speak for Kenya all over the world. When informed of his smashing victory, Mboya rejoiced, "Tomorrow we enter a new era. . . . Let us not become arrogant and racial. . . . Suspicions and fears are unfounded. . . . Let us get down, roll up our sleeves and make Kenya the land of progress, peace and prosperity."

But before they could proceed with that dream, there was some unfinished business to attend to—freedom for Jomo Kenyatta, acknowledged by all rival parties as the true national leader. Despite considerable evidence that Kenyatta's conviction for leading the Mau Mau rebellion was unjust, British Governor-General Sir Patrick Renison refused to act. "Jomo Kenyatta is a leader to darkness and death," he cried.

When Mboya and James Gichuru of the Kenya African National Union, the majority party, and Ronald Ngala and Masindi Muliro of the rival minority, the Kenya African Democratic Union, were summoned to Government House one evening, they thought that Governor-General Renison wanted to confer with them on a timetable for Kenya's independence and other plans for the future. Instead, he came in with a transistor radio and turned on the 9 o'clock news. "Gentlemen," he said, "I have made a statement which I want you to listen to." The broadcast began with the statement that Jomo Kenyatta would not be released until the new government was working well and the security risk presented by returning Mau Mau leaders could be contained. "His return presents a danger to the economy and administration and our whole constitutional progress toward early independence."

Then he snapped off the radio dial. "Well, gentlemen, what do you think of my statement?"

"There's no use asking us because it's already published," Mboya returned glumly. "The Kenya African National Union will not form a government until Jomo Kenyatta is released."

"How can we allow his return at this crucial time?" Renison asked. "He's been in jail or in exile for nine years. We don't even know what he is thinking."

"You have only to fly to Lodwar and talk to him," Mboya snapped.

Without a government, Kenya began to go downhill like a car without a driver. White farmers and white and Asian businessmen became worried, and there was the threat of economic chaos. Renison tried to save the situation by patching together a government from the minority Kenya African Democratic Union Party and the New Kenya Party, representing whites and Asians. Speaking for the majority KANU, Mboya dismissed them as puppets of the British.

In the midst of all this political maneuvering, Mboya had to find time for other concerns. In April he flew to New York, where he addressed an African Freedom Day Rally at Hunter College, met with other African leaders who were also visiting and conferred with President Kennedy and John Diefenbaker, the Prime Minister of Canada. He was, as usual, also successful in raising a great amount of money for African causes.

Mboya went back to fight a threatened Communist takeover of African labor organizations. Refusing to be bullied or coerced at trade union conferences in Casablanca and in Dakar, Mboya stood firmly opposed to the new colonialism of Communists entering through the back door of Africa as the British, French and others departed through the front door.

When he returned to Kenya, events were moving swiftly. Jomo Kenyatta was finally released in August, 1961. There was much curiosity and apprehension, for the "Old Man," "Mzee," as his followers affectionately called him, was well over seventy. One newspaper reports his standing up in front of a meeting attired in a jacket with leopard-skin lapels. Suddenly, he tore it off, flexed his powerful muscles in front of the crowd and asked, "Am I old?" "No!" they roared back.

Indeed, he seemed younger and stronger than ever, and his politics turned out to be more middle-of-the-road than anyone, black or white, had expected. In a speech in the highlands region before white farmers who had been terrorized by the Mau Mau he said, "There is no society of angels, black, brown or white. We are human beings, and as such we are bound to make mistakes. If I have done a mistake to you, it is for you to forgive me. If you have done a mistake to me, it is for me to forgive you."

On April 12, 1962, Jomo Kenyatta became Prime Minister in a soon-to-be-independent Kenya, and Tom Mboya, who had continued in his post as Secretary-General of the Kenya Federation of Labour even though he was an elected representative in the Legislative Council, resigned to become Minister of Labour. Shortly thereafter, a wave of strikes hit Kenya. Most observers believed them to be instigated by Oginga-Odinga and other former associates of Mboya and financed by money from the Soviet Union and Red China. Mboya met the threat with firmness, warning that no country as poor as Kenya could allow its economy to be deliberately crippled and that the government might have to declare strikes illegal.

In the midst of all the feverish activity in preparation for independence, Africa's most eligible bachelor found time to get married. The bride was twenty-two-year-old Pamela Odede, daughter of an old associate of Kenyatta who had been among the first Africans in the old Legislative Council and among the first to be arrested and detained in the early days of the Emergency. Mboya had met her again when she had joined the first student airlift from Nairobi. She had earned a degree in art from Makerere University College in Uganda, and had gone on to get her B.A. in sociology from Western College for Women in Oxford, Ohio.

The ceremony took place at St. Peter Clavers Church in Nairobi, and Pope John XXIII wired the newlyweds his blessings. The guests included Jomo Kenyatta, Governor-General Sir Patrick Renison and some 2,000 others, distinguished and unknown, invited and uninvited. Guests in formal attire mixed with villagers in full ceremonial dress, the latter chanting the age-old ceremonial rites. A women's delegation presented Pamela with many traditional Luo gifts, including a handmade clay pot for her husband's water. The father of the bride later announced that, according to custom, Tom had paid him a bride price of sixteen cows. "It would have been twelve if I had been kind," he said with a smile, "or twenty-four if I had been harsh. No woman is worth more than twenty-four cattle."

The newlyweds visited Israel on their honeymoon, but the Mboyas were no ordinary tourists. The new husband was on a mission from the Kenya Federation of Labor to inspect the Israeli cooperative movement run by the Jewish labor federation, Histadrut. Mboya arranged for joint KFL-Histadrut sponsorship of a cooperative chain of retail stores, a wholesale supply organization, a construction company and various farming and fishing cooperatives throughout Kenya. He also negotiated loans from Histadrut, and outlined plans for credit cooperatives to free people from moneylenders. Mboya was inspired by the Israelis' "fanatical spirit of dedication to build a homeland" and the tremendous pride both young and old took in national progress. At the end of a ten-day whirl of activity, he kissed Pam good-bye and jetted to London to meet Jomo Kenyatta for a conference on Kenya's approaching independence.

At last that great day arrived. On December 12, 1963, a crowd of a quarter of a million jubilant people gathered in the 195-

acre Uhuru Stadium in Nairobi. At one end stood two tall flagpoles
symbolically topped with spears. The British flag, the Union Jack,
flew from one; the other was empty. Kenya's first Prime Minister,
Jomo Kenyatta, resplendent in a monkey-skin cloak and beaded
hat and carrying a silver-handled fly whisk, presented Kenya's
new flag to a contingent of Boy Scouts. It was black for the people,
red for the blood shed for independence and green for the land,
with thin white lines interspersed to show that the flag represented
all Kenyans.

At midnight the blinding battery of floodlights was switched off
and the stadium became black and silent. In the dark the band
played "God Save the Queen" and the Union Jack was hauled down.
Suddenly, the lights illuminated the scene. The band struck up
Kenya's national anthem, and the new flag was slowly hoisted on
the second flagpole. When it reached the top and began to flutter
in the breeze, people cheered and screamed and wept. The sky
exploded in a shower of silver, red and purple as a fireworks display expressed the soaring joy of Kenyans at the birth of their
country. Tribal drums beat out throbbing rhythms, and 1,200
dancers took over the floor of the stadium. A few minutes later
the news arrived that a team of climbers had ascended Mount
Kenya, planted a flag and lit flares that made the sacred mountain
glow like a ball of fire.

For several days the distinguished guests, including Prince Philip,
husband of Queen Elizabeth, attended gala balls, garden parties,
outdoor receptions and private parties. One alert photographer
caught a shot of Pamela Mboya, wife of the Minister of Justice and
Constitutional Affairs in the new government, doing a dance they
promptly labeled "the Uhuru Twist."

When the joyous celebrations were over, the leaders of the new
country and its citizens had to take stock. At independence Kenya
had a land area about the size of Texas, inhabited by 8.3 million
Africans, 66,000 whites and 300,000 Arabs and Indians. Everyone
had his own idea of what freedom would bring. "The simple
peasant may think of Uhuru in terms of farm credits, more food,

schools for his children. The office clerk may see it as meaning promotion to an executive job. The apprentice may interpret it as a chance to qualify as a technician, the schoolboy as a chance for a scholarship overseas, the sick person as the provision of better hospital facilities, the aged worker as the hope of pensions and old-age security," Mboya explained.

But none of this could come about unless a new slogan were adopted. *Uhuru* had been gained; now it was time for *Harambee*—"Let's all pull together"! For Kenya had many serious problems to solve, and now that it was independent, it could no longer rely on the British or blame them. No one knew this better than the man who in December, 1964, was appointed to take charge of economic planning and development for the new country—Tom Mboya.

First, there was the touchy problem of the land. About 4,000 white farmers had taken about one-quarter of the arable land; about 5½ million Africans lived on the rest. However, the farms in the "White Highlands" produced the coffee, sisal and pyrethrum that accounted for 80 per cent of Kenya's exports. The government could not afford to break up these large farms to give them back to the Africans. On the one hand, the fears of the whites had to be soothed; on the other, Africans who had suffered hunger and insult for so long had to be persuaded to wait. Mboya obtained from England a thirty-year loan of $150 million to buy up unused land and farms from whites who were pulling out. Some 20,000 Africans settled on these vast acres which had been white plantations, but the problem was far from solved. According to a 1965 report in *The New York Times*, the clock had been put back fifty years in the "White Highlands." "Combine-harvesters and tractors have been replaced by hand axes and primitive hoes. Trees are being felled. Fine-wooled sheep are being replaced by bad breeds or goats." "A political necessity but an economic disaster," was the conclusion. However, planner Mboya and Minister of Agriculture Brian McKenzie, Kenya's only white Cabinet member, concentrated on education for farmers, demonstration projects and the formation of cooperatives. Latest reports show that Kenya's agriculture has started on the long, hard climb back. The next problem is to take care of the 100,000 African families who are still clamoring for the return of tribal lands.

Kenya encountered another serious problem when the government tried to work out its multi-racial policy. Many of the whites in Kenya refused to take a chance on being ruled by the African majority and went back to England. Yet Mboya noted with joy that during his 1963 election campaign "there were many Europeans doing the run-of-the-mill work of addressing envelopes, distributing leaflets, driving cars and so forth. When it was all over, we had a celebration party. As I looked around the room and saw the happy, jostling crowd of people of all races, I knew that here was the spirit of the new, nonracial Kenya the Government aims to build."

But Mboya backed a policy of Africanization of the civil service, even when it led to mass firings of whites. We need "loyal, disciplined, self-sacrificing" public servants, he insisted.

An even more serious problem is posed by the almost 200,000 Asians who have had a virtual monopoly on Kenya's small businesses. Many of these Indians and Pakistanis knew no other home but Kenya, as their ancestors came from Asia in the late 1800s to work on British railroads. Many others came more recently for better economic opportunity in Africa. A tightly knit community, most Asians chose British citizenship rather than Kenyan citizenship after independence. Can a country allow most of its business to be run by aliens, Planning Minister Mboya asked. Accordingly, work permits and business licenses have been refused, causing panic among the Asians. "This [Indian] says he is a Kenyan but wants to keep an emergency exit [the British passport] which I as an African citizen do not have," Mboya pointed out. The real test of sincerity, he believed, is whether the person cuts his outside ties to become a citizen of Kenya. There is no such thing as dual citizenship, Mboya maintained. "Is he in the melting pot with us?" Certainly Mboya would have admitted there is discrimination against those who have not become citizens, but "a true Kenyan must be entitled to some degree of privilege in his mother country."

Another of Kenya's problems is one which its leadership does not look upon as a problem. After eight months of independence, Jomo Kenyatta proclaimed Kenya a one-party state to overcome, he explained, the divisions among fifty different tribal groups. Tom Mboya agreed wholeheartedly. You cannot transplant the English or French or American democratic system onto African soil and expect it will flourish under very different conditions, he maintained. In the early stages of independence Kenya cannot afford the luxury of disagreement; everyone must pull together against the great common enemies of ignorance and disease. A country can be democratic. Mboya believed, without an opposition party.

An ever-present threat to the security of Kenya is the possibility of a Communist takeover. Led by former Vice-President Oginga-Odinga, the movement has been well financed by the Russians and Red Chinese. Arms have been smuggled in, student activists trained abroad and wildcat strikes and illegal land grabs encouraged to undermine the government. At one point Kenyatta had to swallow his pride and call in British troops to overcome a threatened military coup. Another time he had to expel Communist diplomats and journalists suspected of guiding anti-government activities.

Kenyatta finally asked Mboya to draft a Constitution which would freeze out the Vice-President. At the same time, he requested Mboya to write a manifesto on "African Socialism." The result was *African Socialism and Its Application to Planning in Kenya*, which Kenyatta has called his "economic Bible." In it Mboya rejected both 19th-century capitalism and 20th-century communism as models for African development.

On the future, Mboya wrote: "Africa has been cutting new trails. Anyone who has hacked his way through a forest undergrowth knows that you cannot go far without some scratches and even some blood on your legs. Too many journalists and sensational writers have concentrated on these scratches and, getting this scene totally out of perspective, have interpreted Africa as a continent of violence and bloodshed. Being patient and unusually good-humored people, we are amused that this should be the view of white men who have started two world wars and burned up thousands of civilians with atomic bombs, and even now crouch in terror lest their opponents in the East or West may loose their huge nuclear armories in their direction. Is this what they call freedom? We in Africa are confident that . . . we are heading in the right direction along our new trail. Our road is a classless socialism, based on Ujamaa, the extended family. Our goal is to share the blessings of a richly endowed continent among all its inhabitants; to make a reality of the brotherhood of 'the extended family' in a United States of Africa; and to spread this feeling of kinship further through our international policy of . . . friendship with all nations. We are happy in the conviction that before many more years have passed we will be showing the rest of the world what freedom really means."

An elder statesman at thirty-eight, Mboya continued in the key job of Minister for Planning and Economic Development. His concerns were plans for self-help projects, securing foreign investments, setting up training programs for doctors and teachers, building hospitals and schools, beginning a youth corps for national service and meeting with other African leaders for joint action to fulfill his lifelong dream of a United States of Africa. His work in building up a nation may not have been as spectacular or exciting as the fight for independence, but it will have great long-run effects.

As Jomo Kenyatta approached 80, there was, naturally, much speculation about a successor. Many saw Mboya as the model of a new breed of African leader—intelligent, well-spoken, politically sophisticated and able to inspire national unity among Kenyans regardless of their different backgrounds. Others felt that Kenyans still cling to their tribal loyalties and that a Luo like Mboya could not aspire to the Presidency of a Kikuyu-dominated country. Speculation on Mboya's future was shattered July 5, 1969. As he walked out of a drugstore in downtown Nairobi, an assassin jumped out of an automobile and fired three shots. Mboya slumped to the ground;

people flew screaming for cover. In the confusion the auto sped away without positive identification of the gunman or his two accomplices. A short while later Mboya was pronounced dead on arrival at Nairobi Hospital.

Historians often speculate on "what might have been." At 38 Tom Mboya still had a big part to play in the future of Kenya and in the future of all of Africa. Former U.S. Ambassador William Attwood described him as "cool, reserved, modern-minded, pragmatic and hardworking." An old rival, Achieng Oneko of the opposition Kenya People's Union party, exclaimed in tears, "This is not a political assassination. There is no question of parties here. He belonged to us all." But Jomo Kenyatta, mourning for his talented colleague, best summed up the senseless destruction of Tom Mboya as "a loss to Kenya, to Africa, and the world."

SUGGESTED FURTHER READING

Chu, Daniel and Skinner, Elliot. *A Glorious Age in Africa.* Garden City: Doubleday & Co., 1965 (Zenith Books).

Davidson, Basil. *Africa: History of a Continent.* New York: Macmillan Co., 1966.

————. *A Guide to African History.* Garden City: Doubleday & Co., 1965 (Zenith Books).

Dobler, Lavinia and Brown, William A. *Great Rulers of the African Past.* Garden City: Doubleday & Co., 1965 (Zenith Books).

Gardner, Brian. *The Quest for Timbucktoo.* New York: Harcourt, Brace, and World, Inc., 1968.

Gatheru, R. Mugo. *Child of Two Worlds.* Garden City: Doubleday & Co., 1965 (Anchor Books).

Gunther, John. *Inside Africa.* New York: Harper & Bros., 1955.

Rake, Alan. *Tom Mboya, Young Man of New Africa.* Garden City: Doubleday & Co., 1962.

Roberts, John S. *A Land Full of People: Life in Kenya Today.* New York: Frederick A. Praeger, 1967.

Savage, Katharine. *The Story of Africa South of the Sahara.* Walck, 1961.

Shinnie, Margaret, *Ancient African Kingdoms.* New York: St. Martin's Press, 1965.

INDEX

MANSA MUSA

QUEEN NZINGA

SAMUEL AJAYI CROWTHER

MOSHOESHOE

TOM MBOYA

ABOUT THE AUTHORS

Florence T. Polatnick was born in Manhattan and attended Walton High School in the Bronx. She received her B.A. from Brooklyn College, her M.A. from the New School for Social Research and her M.S. from Yeshiva University. She now lives in Plainview, New York.

Alberta L. Saletan was born in Asheville, North Carolina, and attended Fieldston School in Riverdale, New York. She received her B.A. and M.A. from the University of Wisconsin and did additional graduate work at Columbia and Yeshiva universities. She now lives in Roslyn Heights, New York.

The careers of Florence Polatnick and Alberta Saletan have been so remarkably parallel that it is curious that their paths did not cross sooner. Both received graduate degrees in economics and did editorial work in that field, then retired to raise families. Active in school affairs and many civic and humanitarian organizations, both then decided to return to work as teachers. They met after beginning their teaching careers in Syosset, New York, and fruitful professional collaboration led to a joint sabbatical leave. The result was several publications for teachers and students in African studies classes and the idea for this book. They are currently devoting their extracurricular time to in-service workshops and courses and research for a new book.

DATE DUE

GAYLORD   PRINTED IN U.S.A.